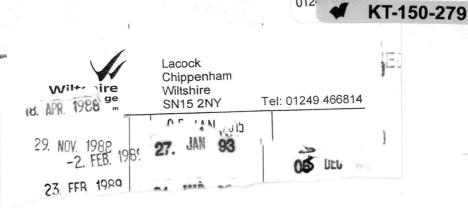

Farm Animal Welfare

Farm Animal Welfare
Cattle, Pigs and Poultry

David Sainsbury

COLLINS
8 Grafton Street, London W1

Collins Professional and Technical Books
William Collins Sons & Co. Ltd
8 Grafton Street, London W1X 3LA

First published in Great Britain by
Collins Professional and Technical Books 1986

Distributed in the United States of America
by Sheridan House, Inc.

Copyright © David Sainsbury 1986

British Library Cataloguing in Publication Data
Sainsbury, David
Farm animal welfare.
1. Livestock
I. Title
636.08'3   SF61

ISBN 0-00-383157-4

Typeset by Columns of Reading
Printed and bound in Great Britain by
MacKays of Chatham, Kent

Contents

Acknowledgements

One of the pleasures of writing a book is that it gives an author the opportunity of acknowledging those investigators in the subject who have contributed to the existing knowledge and whose work he quotes. Under this heading I wish to express grateful thanks to Dr. Marian Dawkins of Oxford University, Drs Ian Duncan and Barry Hughes of the Poultry Research Centre, Edinburgh, Dr. Bob Baldwin of the Institute of Animal Physiology, Babraham and Professor John Webster of the Bristol Veterinary School. I also wish to express my sincerest thanks to Mr. Jan Cermak and colleagues in the Ministry of Agriculture, Fisheries and Food for the use of certain diagrams, and my gratitude for their valuable work towards the better welfare of cattle; and to Dr. Mandy Hill at the Gleadthorpe Experimental Husbandry Farm of the Ministry of Agriculture for her extensive investigations over several years, with special reference to poultry work on 'alternative systems'. Also for many years agriculture has been indebted to the Scottish Farm Buildings Investigation Unit at Aberdeen, founded by Mr. David Soutar, and now continuing its good work under the direction of Dr. James Bruce, with welfare orientated investigations being pursued particularly by Dr. Mike Baxter. Certain diagrams, that is, the Craibstone Ark, the Pitmillan farrowing unit and the Monopitch calf house originated from the SFBIU. I am also grateful for the permission of the West of Scotland College of Agriculture to use Figures 13.4, 13.5 and 13.6 which show cattle handling and isolation facilities and a bull pen. In the text I have quoted from the valuable investigations of Professor Wood-Gush of Edinburgh University, Dr. Martin Seabrook of Reading University, Mr. S.A. Edwards of the Terrington Experimental Husbandry Farm in Cambridgeshire and, abroad, Professors Ekesbo and Dantzer and their colleagues. Thanks are also due to Mr. Roger Ewbank, Director of the Universities Federation for Animal Welfare, for supporting many animal welfare investigations and to Mr. Paul Carnell for his invaluable study on the economics of alternative husbandry systems.

Finally, my brother Peter Sainsbury, Dairy Husbandry Officer in Devon, generously assisted me with the material in the chapter on dairy cattle.

It gives me the greatest pleasure to thank Mr. Julian Grover of Collins Professional and Technical Books for his constant support, together with Miss Margaret KcKean for her invaluable help with the manuscript.

Preface

The aim of this book is the entirely practical one of attempting to consider the field of farm animal welfare as a whole and to give recommendations for the provision of good animal welfare in our present state of knowledge and belief. The animal welfare field is currently a battleground between two extremes. On one side are the extreme 'welfarists' who believe that animals should be given conditions similar to those they perceive are their natural habitats, whilst on the other side are the extreme 'intensivists' who believe that the only standard we should be concerned with is that of production, and if an animal produces adequately there can be little or nothing wrong with its welfare.

Both views appear to many to be difficult to sustain. When our domesticated livestock are given natural, free range to their activities, serious problems often arise with management and disease whilst productivity can fall dramatically and losses by predators can, on occasions, be extensive. There is also no evidence that production has any direct relationship with welfare. Aside from the livestock welfare aspects, intensive farming may be of questionable economics whilst the operations tend to be divorced from local agriculture and are often a nuisance to the local inhabitants, principally due to smell from the slurry and the animals.

I do not see any reason why livestock rearing should not be highly productive and yet also follow conditions of rearing that satisfy reasonable welfare codes. In this book the emphasis is on methods that follow a middle course between the two extremes. The scientific evidence demarcating good and bad welfare systems is largely absent, so it is our task to keep animals in such ways that satisfy the general consensus of informed opinion. I also believe very strongly that livestock rearing can perhaps be the most satisfying of all occupations, but it is not the high-pressure, intensive methods that usually provide the satisfaction but the less intensive systems that attempt to be in harmony with the whole agriculture of the area.

In considering the welfare aspect of livestock rearing methods, it is essential to look at the whole management of the animals so that the end result gives a balanced system which is in harmony with its surroundings. As the first chapters in this book explain, this covers a substantial number of factors ranging from the climatic environment, hygiene and health, to the detailed design of the lying, feeding and exercising areas. It is recognised that there is no perfect system for each animal and, indeed, every system has its good and bad points, I hope, however, that the reader will be able to appreciate from the practical information in the book that many fine systems of management exist which are economic in both capital and running costs, provide acceptable conditions both for the animals and their stockmen, and can give a return on investment which is second to none.

1 Introduction

In the past thirty years or so there has been increasing concern in the United Kingdom, and many other parts of the world, with some of the methods used to raise farm livestock. This concern has arisen for a substantial number of reasons which are summarised as follows:

1. Many systems greatly restrict the movement of the animals – such as poultry or pigs kept in cages – and this is felt to be inhumane, being too far removed from their natural habitat.
2. Methods which restrict movement excessively and also crowd the animals tightly often produce the cruel effect of animals abusing each other and indulging in cannibalism and vices such as tail-biting and feather-pecking.
3. Many systems do not allow the animals the comfort of bedding. Stock may be confined on concrete, metal or plastic flooring, sometimes slatted or perforated. The comfort and humanity of such arrangements is often questioned.
4. Environmental control is often insufficient for the comfort of the animal and may in fact be for the benefit of productivity at the expense of welfare.
5. Many modern systems put the inspection of the animals at risk. For example, it is very difficult adequately to inspect huge numbers of animals kept together in pens or yards without them being separated into smaller groups, and having animals stacked in cages up to six tiers high makes adequate lighting and inspection difficult.
6. Many husbandry systems require an excessive or continuous use of drugs or vaccines to maintain the animals' good health. This is expensive, may eventually lead, ironically, to a breakdown in health, and can be injurious to human health.
7. Total reliance on mechanical environmental control and food

and water provision can be of great danger to the animals' welfare if the system fails.

8. Highly restrictive systems may prevent the animals grooming or preening themselves, both of which are inherent requirements for welfare and health and therefore something they should never be denied.

9. It should be inherent in all livestock systems that the animals are separated from the waste products of respiration and excretion. Several modern systems consistently fail to do this and produce problems with management, health and welfare that often defeat the finest stockman.

Unfortunately in the emotion associated with farm animal welfare the very term 'welfare' has become distorted in meaning. It has been associated by many only with limited aspects of the behaviour of the animals, implying that it is sufficient merely to allow them plenty of movement and to keep them under conditions which are considered roughly to correspond to what is believed to be the animal's natural habitat. These factors are obviously worthy of consideration, but welfare should be very much more than that.

Good health is perhaps the most important factor of all, but with a number of the systems advocated by the welfarists (and for reasons which they seem unable to understand) there is a considerable risk of the animals being subjected to far less healthy conditions. The notion that intensification is bad and free-range is good is a delightfully naïve concept which deserves critical scrutiny. The true facts in practice may be altogether different. Animals under free-range conditions can suffer considerable harm and stress from bad weather at both ends of the weather spectrum, and good farming practice has been at pains for many years to provide an ever-improving level of protection from such stresses.

In recent years we have learned much about the physiological needs of animals and it would be quite illogical to ignore this very important information that has a bearing not merely on productivity and health, but also on the welfare of farm animals. Any alternative system must incorporate the fruits of such knowledge in its design. Likewise, on the health front the advances have been equally phenomenal, and no system of keeping animals should sacrifice these benefits; regrettably, many alternative systems pay little heed to such matters in their somewhat myopic determination to provide a natural environment. It must be appreciated that the farm animal has become much more productive in recent years, due partly to the factors already mentioned associated with better environment and health, but also due to improvements in nutrition and breeding. It would be illogical to reject these, otherwise we could very well be guilty of replacing one form of supposed cruelty with another, which would only emerge later, after use of the 'alternative' chosen.

What is good welfare?

Turning from the negative to the positive aspects of animal welfare, the UK Codes of Recommendation for the Welfare of Livestock define the basic requirements for good welfare as:
'. . . a husbandry system appropriate to the health and, so far as is practicable, the behavioural needs of the animals and a high standard of stockmanship'. Some of these essentials are easy enough to follow whilst others are much more difficult. A summary of the needs is as follows:

1. Comfort and shelter.
2. Readily accessible fresh water and a diet to maintain the animals in full health and vigour.
3. Freedom of movement.
4. The company of other animals, particularly of like kind.
5. The opportunity to exercise most normal patterns of behaviour.
6. Light during hours of daylight and lighting readily available to enable the animals to be inspected at any time.
7. Flooring which neither harms the animals nor causes undue strain.
8. The prevention and rapid diagnosis and treatment of vice, injury, parasitic infection and disease.
9. The avoidance of unnecessary mutilation.
10. Emergency arrangements to cover outbreaks of fire, the breakdown of essential mechanical services and the disruption of supplies.

Stockmanship in particular is difficult to define but is certainly a key factor, because no matter how otherwise acceptable a system may be in principle, without competent and diligent stockmanship the welfare of the animals can never be adequately catered for. We all have our own ideas of what good stockmanship means, and we know that able stockmanship is in large measure art rather than science. Nevertheless it is clearly essential that a thorough training is available. Modern intensive husbandry is full of complex equipment and methods, and training is essential for its proper application. Great effort should be put into the provision of this in the coming years.

Every species of livestock that is kept by man on the farm, or is otherwise reared and confined for the ultimate benefit of man, is threatened in one way or another if the Codes are not followed. As intensification has developed, the parts of the Codes which deal with the limitation of movement, or of the natural behaviour of animals, are those which have caused the greatest concern but we should be fully aware of the fact that the more traditional methods of rearing have hazards which can be equally serious. For example, the rearing of livestock outdoors may be accompanied by serious diseases, especially parasitism, whilst diet has its problems, and diagnosis of ill health is sometimes difficult. The free-range animal or bird may suffer markedly from bad weather conditions, the attention of predators or a build-up of infection on bird-sick land. Semi-intensive systems, once so popular for keeping domestic fowl, can probably claim to produce the highest disease incidence of all systems, and also present great difficulties with high labour costs, poor standards of hygiene of the eggs and also some behavioural problems. Animals kept on slatted floors suffer the greatest restriction of their movement and the most unnatural and barren of surroundings, but they can be adequately fed, watered and housed. Let us therefore be under no delusions; the moment we take into our control the management of livestock there are great welfare responsibilities, though their nature will vary enormously between the management systems.

It is becoming clear that acceptable scientific answers to what constitutes good and bad welfare are unlikely to be found in the foreseeable future, if ever. A wide range of neurological, biochemical and ethological investigations have been undertaken with a view to determining welfare stresses, and many more are currently in progress, but the results have been largely unfruitful in yielding answers with practical conclusions and we still cannot say, for example, whether chicken within cramped multi-bird cages are suffering real distress. The attitude could be taken that we must wait for research to give us a definite answer before any legislative moves are made to give mandatory approval or rejection of housing arrangements. Such a delay is probably unacceptable for a number of reasons. There is a widespread and quite genuine disquiet about the extreme methods used in factory farming, and the view is expressed that, if there are doubts on the issues, one should give the benefit of the doubts to the animals and therefore legislate for those methods that are broadly acceptable. Also, there is considerable pressure from the politicians and 'direct-action' extremists. I think it is highly undesirable we should let the initiative in the animal welfare debate come from these two latter sections of the community whose lack of practical knowledge on the subject of animal husbandry and welfare is often profound. There is a real danger that we could be forced by extremists to revert to husbandry systems that caused much more distress and suffering to animals in a different way and raised production costs a lot more into the bargain.

Modern intensive animal husbandry, with its massive conglomerations of livestock, manages them on a knife edge, as it were, between success and failure. There is little joy in being involved in such enterprises. It is a tragedy if we do find ourselves in this position, when it is in our grasp to produce almost completely healthy stock since by and large the acute and epidemic infections and contagions are conquered. This is, of course, still possible even with these modern systems; for example, the best broiler growers using the 'all-in, all-out' principle in almost clinically clean houses chart up consistent losses of no more than 2 or 3 per cent. But most 'factory farming' is not like this, and the endeavour seems to be to accept a background of infection with a constant addition of drugs and vaccines as part of the act. Sites may be too big to depopulate, buildings too badly built to keep properly clean and disinfected, and excreta accumulates around the animals in their litter-less environment.

It should be stressed too that, allied to the welfare problems of the animals, there is a concern in the public mind at the consumption of animal products which have been derived from animals which have consumed quantities of drugs and growth

promoters. There have been allegations that the residues from
such materials in the meat or eggs may be harmful; also that the
continual use of such substances will lead to the production of
strains of pathogenic organisms resistant to therapeutic agents.
There is a strong and constantly nagging feeling, too, that it is
wrong to have husbandry systems and housing methods that
cannot work perfectly well without the constant aid of drugs.
That this is so is generally agreed, although it may have no
direct bearing on livestock welfare. It does, however, have an
indirect connection insofar as it is a generally expressed truism
that *any livestock enterprise that can only function with the
constant administration of drugs will eventually fail.*

The philosophy of the alternatives

Clearly there is no need to accept methods of 'factory farming' if
we can find alternatives which in the long run may have great
advantages. The questions that must be asked are:

1. Can we keep animals economically without a high degree of
   confinement? Can they be as productive and appear to exist
   in a more 'natural' environment?
2. Is it necessary to have diets constantly fortified with drugs
   and other agents to promote growth and counteract infections?
3. Can we keep animals in small numbers, more closely
   associated with the land, thus avoiding difficulties of dung
   disposal, of public nuisance, and of excessive build-up of
   pathogens, and possibly allowing greater use of home-grown
   products in the feeding of the stock?

It has always been a main argument of the intensive farmer
that whilst it would be fine in principle to return to the ways of
our traditional farming forbears, it is quite impossible to do so
economically and still feed people in the manner to which they
are now accustomed, and at a price which they can afford.
These are powerful arguments but they may be countered by
giving the following replies:

1. To every system that causes concern because of its restric-
   tions there are one or more alternatives. In some cases the
   changes have already taken place; for example, laying birds

can now be kept satisfactorily in straw yards, deep litter, 'aviaries', 'percheries', and other ways that the ever-ingenious farmer has evolved as alternatives. Calves formerly kept in crates for veal may now be housed in deeply strawed yards, and sows in tethers or stalls can thrive just as well in kennels or yards.

2. It may sometimes appear on a superficial estimate that 'alternatives' are much more expensive. This is certainly not always the case. On average they appear to involve a production cost of about 20% more in the case of battery chicken, and in other cases either less than this or even no greater cost at all. If alternatives are looked at more carefully and in particular if not only the capital but also the depreciation and maintenance costs are examined, the picture may be very different and the simpler system may show up much more favourably.

It is for these reasons that the agricultural industry is itself moving forward and seeking more economical alternatives to the 'factory-farm', and it is, in fact, finding them. These are described in later chapters.

There are more features in modern intensive animal husbandry than welfare to cause us concern. For example, attention is drawn to the 'nuisance' that may be created by large conglomerations of livestock, arising chiefly from the smells of the stock and their bedding, but above all from the excreta, especially if this is produced in slurry form. This latter material, being anaerobic and unlike the traditional farmyard manure, has led to a large number of legal tussles, and many units have been closed down because of the nuisance created near human habitations. It is, of course, a great tragedy when the muck is a liability rather than an asset, but then, many huge intensive units are really an anachronism in the countryside. To them is applied the term 'factory-farm', as they have no relationship with the land on which they sit or that around them. The food for the animals comes from elsewhere, much of it perhaps being imported from the other side of the world. The animals themselves may also be bred elsewhere and the muck may have to be disposed of some distance away, perhaps under great difficulty at certain times of the year.

Unit size and depopulation

Economists who look at this question dispassionately have long stated from their analyses of the situation that 'small is beautiful' when it comes to livestock units. From the health aspect also the same basic concept holds. A preferred criterion in planning the size of a unit is that it should be small enough to be regularly emptied of stock and thereafter be completely cleaned, disinfected and rested. This procedure is also of great benefit to the stockmen who can be given a pause from their daily chores. It is a perfect procedure if it is always followed in the case of young animals, although it is virtually impossible to achieve in practice with the breeding animal, except in poultry. Production is also favourably affected by frequent and careful division of the animals within a unit and up-to-date, scientific figures on this are given elsewhere. With young animals that are settling down to life in the outside world and are developing some gradual immunity to the local disease challenges, it is a great help if the age spread is minimal, to prevent the older animals challenging the younger and breaking their immunity before it has developed properly. A further advantage, if the animals are of uniform size as well as age, is that there will be a minimum challenge or pressure, the animals will grow together and can hopefully come into the unit and go out again over a very short space of time. Hence modest numbers are a great assistance in achieving successful 'all-in, all-out' policies.

An example of the effect of numbers of animals in a unit is given in Table 1.1, summarising a pig production survey by Bakx (1979). A difference of approximately 9% in growth rate in favour of the small unit over the larger is a potentially enormous one, even without allowing for the inevitably greater incidence of disease in the larger unit. I have given several other examples elsewhere (Sainsbury & Sainsbury, 1979) and concluded from such scientific evidence as there is, but more especially on the evidence of current practical and clinical experience, that the following numbers are probably fair proposals as to the maximum number of livestock of various species that there should be on one unit:

Dairy cows	200
Beef cattle	1 000

Breeding pigs	500
Fattening pigs	3 000
Sheep	1 000
Commercial laying poultry	70 000
Breeding poultry	3 000
Broiler chicken	200 000

It is worthy of emphasis that if smaller units give the best productivity, the most favourable food conversion efficiency and the lowest incidence of disease, then it is they that make the best use of the world's resources on these criteria alone. There are, of course, the others, such as the benefits of good use of waste products and the greater likelihood of maximum use of locally grown produce, which will further tip the balance in the identical direction. Thus, from every aspect, the smaller unit is likely to favour the welfare of both the animals and their stockmen.

Table 1.1 Relationship between size of units and the growth rate of fattening pigs (from Bakx, 1979)

No. of places per unit	Growth rate (g/day)
‹100	680
100–150	668
›150	635

All evidence appears to point in the direction of 'small is beautiful' so far as livestock is concerned. The benefits in growth rate shown here are as much as 9% in favour of the small unit.

The search for simpler arrangements

Because of the complexity and high capital cost of the modern intensive house, and because of the problems mentioned, there has been a determined search for simpler, less stressful techniques. By and large these alternatives already exist and the following criteria are those in broad outline which are sought for the alternative arrangements, which should suit the welfare of man and animals and create the proper harmony of the livestock industry.

The livestock enterprise should be of a size that can be managed by no more than four people. A substantial proportion of the fodder should be locally grown, whilst the manure from the animals should all be usable locally; if it is in solid or semi-solid form, mixed with suitable bedding material such as straw or wood shavings, this is ideal. Wherever possible, bedding should be obtained locally, if not from the farm itself. The enterprise should have management supervised by a specialist stockman. Wherever possible animal housing systems will be used that give the animals generous space allowances, keep them in smallish groups and do not rely on artificial environmental control. Under these circumstances dire emergencies caused by break-down or failure in the electrical supply are far less likely and the stockman is more likely to be a manager of stock than a repairer of equipment. Details are given elsewhere of the various housing systems that can successfully be used as alternatives. It is quite possible that such housing systems can have a measure of adaptability so that the type of stock within them may be changed from time to time without too great an expense.

A considerable bonus to be expected in this type of housing is an improved health status. Spreading the stock through smaller units will reduce the disease challenge and will more easily enable the site to be cleared for the all-in, all-out policy required. Any contagious disease that does crop up will be likely to spread more slowly, or not at all, in this form of 'divided' or 'isolation' housing.

References

Bakx, J.A.E. (1979) 'Onderzoek op Varkensmestbedrijven van integratiegroepen'. *Bedrijfsontwikkeling* 10, 375–388

Sainsbury, D., and Sainsbury, P. (1979) *Livestock Health and Housing*. London: Baillière Tindall Ltd.

2 Stockmanship

Stockmanship is a term frequently used to imply the skilled management and handling of livestock by their attendants. There is no doubt that the correct care of livestock, whatever may be the system under which they are kept, can transcend most other things in the attempt to achieve what is believed to be good welfare. Good stockmen are indeed the 'salt of the earth' – they recognise the contented and the distressed, the satisfied and the hungry, the healthy and the sick, the thriving and the 'bad doers'. The good stockman develops something of a sixth sense which tells him when all is not well in an animal house. He will then react quickly and take appropriate action, such as to provide water where it has run out, call in the veterinary surgeon where there is sickness, isolate the bullied animal where it is distressed, or increase the ventilation where there has been a failure. The dedication of the stockman recognises that he has a 24-hour job for most of the year and of all those in the community who are admired for their skill, he ranks second to none.

The responsibility of the stockman is considerable and under modern intensive farming covers many facets of management. As well as his required ability with stock there has to be an understanding of the mechanical equipment which will range from ventilation controls, lighting circuits and automatic feeding and watering devices, to the equipment dealing with the disposal of muck, and the highly complex machinery devoted to the milking of cows, and its subsequent cleansing. Most vital equipment is now fitted with an alarm system to warn of failure, and this must be checked regularly to make certain it is in good working order. It is an anomaly that someone should be expected to cater for so much, and to deal with such a diversity of complex items, but is rarely given detailed or indeed any instructions as to how to do so.

Services for the stockman

The facilities for the stockman are often totally inadequate for him to achieve proper efficiency in his demanding job. Managing intensive livestock units calls for a very sharp attention to detail which was not required of the traditional, slower moving, contemplative and philosophical stockman. He now often has great pressure put on him and it is difficult always to keep up the high standards required. Very often the fall-off in results may be traced to a loss of enthusiasm and interest on the part of the stockman due to the excessive number of stock he must care for.

Essentially, his personal requirements are not unduly complicated. There must be a place which is clean and hygienic where he can keep protective clothing and records. Washing facilities for himself and boots, etc., are vital. It will also be necessary to have a decent place to store medicines and other aids to good management. Design of the animal accommodation at every point should give full attention to the stockman's needs. The building should be well lit for inspection purposes, with natural lighting used wherever possible. In recent years a total reliance on artificial lighting has developed which is difficult to justify. In practice, the only livestock for which a control of lighting is necessary for the furtherance of their physiological – largely reproductive – function is poultry. In other cases the control of lighting is only partially needed – as with broilers, to reduce their activity and the risk of vices such as feather-pecking. It is not nearly as pleasant or conducive to good stockmanship to work in a building where nothing can be seen of the outside world. Artificial lighting is rarely as good as natural lighting through much of the day. Just as we shall emphasise the problem of 'boredom' as we believe it may apply to animals, so can this apply also to the stockman. Much more could be done to prevent him becoming more like a robot and less like a stockman with the time to attend to daily chores and the time and the inclination to observe the unusual and take appropriate action. Stockmanship is very much about ensuring a quick reaction to problems.

Seabrook (1984) has shown very well what he has termed the psychological interaction between the stockman and his animals and its influence on performance of livestock. He lists the following factors as indicative of the stockman achieving a good relationship with his stock:

1. Animals have short flight distance.
2. Animals tend to move towards the stockman (some of this may be conditioned learning since they may receive a reward, e.g. extra food).
3. Animals tend to move quickly into the pen or milking parlour.
4. Animals are not restless in the presence of the stockman.
5. Animals are not easily frightened (i.e. not jumpy).
6. Animals defecate less in the presence of the stockman.
7. Stockman touches the animals.
8. Stockman communicates with animals (talking 'to' and talking 'with').
9. Stockman likes being with the animals and spends more of his available time in contact with them.
10. At times of stress stockman touches and communicates with animals more.
11. Man appears as the 'boss' animal but can also accept a more submissive and caring role (i.e. mother substitute).

It thus seems that the stockman should give the animals favourable stimuli when they are with him so that they associate him with pleasant feelings, avoid giving them unfavourable stimuli except in the role of adopting the 'boss' animal position, and at critical points in the animal's life cycle (e.g. cows when calving), give the animals more pleasant stimuli.

Training of stockmen

It is essential for stockmen to be efficiently trained. In the UK, up-to-date and comprehensive courses are provided by the Agricultural Training Board and local education authorities, apart from the important stockmanship element in courses in Livestock Farming at Agricultural Colleges. To encourage the attainment of skills in stockmanship, there should be appropriate financial rewards together with additional inducement, such as officially acceptable certification. It is possible that one of the most effective means of achieving good welfare would be to have a register of licensed stockmen who would be required to be responsible for livestock units. Such a measure might be more economical and fruitful than attempting to enforce welfare by the cumbersome, expensive and complicated processes of the law.

Reference

Seabrook, M.F. (1984) 'The psychological interaction between the stockman and his animals and its influence on performance of pigs and dairy cows.' *Veterinary Record* **115** 84–87.

3 Health and Welfare

Good health is the birthright of every animal that we rear, whether intensively or otherwise. If it becomes diseased we have failed in our duty to the animal and subjected it to a degree of suffering that cannot be readily estimated. Sick animals give an impression of misery which tends to be obvious merely by observation, and if they are in a group they may in addition be subjected to a degree of bullying which may cause severe injury or even their premature death. I believe it is not sufficiently understood by those interested in animal welfare that good health may be the most vital factor of all.

Modern intensive animal rearing systems certainly endeavour to maintain good health but, as stressed earlier, it is arguable that they rely too much on vaccination and medication and too little on good husbandry, hygiene and system management. An animal which is medicated to control disease is not as truly healthy as one which is maintaining health by living in a totally favourable environment. No one has found the perfect word to describe this state, but the term *positive health* has been used and is perhaps a logical expression. Essentially, this means the provision of a complete diet, an environment that is optimal for the animal's physiological needs, comfortable to the animal's senses, in which the animal is secure and free from fear, and with no undue challenge by pathogenic micro-organisms or predators.

We achieve these essentials in a number of ways. The dietary needs are obviously not only the provision of a diet which satisfies the biochemical needs of the animals, but one which also provides a sense of well-being to the animal together with freedom from intestinal pain. Management must also ensure a sufficient area of, and access to feeding points so that animals can reach their feed without undue competition. A correct environment implies the maintenance of the correct temperature, humidity, ventilation, and air movement. Comfort and freedom from fear means that the animals are housed in well-lit accommodation that enables them, and their attendants, to see and be seen by each other.

In the endeavour to obtain good health the first need is to place the animals in a totally clean environment. The best systems of livestock rearing keep the animals in 'all-in, all-out' systems, animals going into the unit all at one time after the buildings, or preferably the whole site, have been emptied. This arrangement prevents the build-up of infection that can readily happen on intensive units, resulting in the place becoming almost unusable as a viable livestock operation. Under such circumstances drugs are not the answer since they are an added expense, drug resistance soon makes itself apparent and, however good the drug may be, it is not really possible for it to eliminate the disease, only to dampen down its effects. Vaccines too may be overcome by the massive challenge, and in any case there are bound to be numerous pathogens that do not have a vaccine to counter them. The great advantage of the 'all-in, all-out' system, together with the highest standard of disinfection, is that it can reduce or even eliminate the whole range of pathogenic micro-organisms if the building is properly attended to.

So important is this subject in the attainment of healthy stock that it is worthy of some detailed consideration. Firstly, it should be emphasised that really good hygiene is of paramount importance in the younger animal that is developing its immunity to disease, whereas the adult has usually got a fair resistance to the local 'potential pathogens'. For the diseases we are really concerned with are not the well-known disorders which are clearly described and relatively easily diagnosed. Many of these have in any case been eliminated, whilst others have known treatments. The serious problems now in intensive animal husbandry are those caused by organisms which are universally present and which in the normal way do no harm. If, however, there is any stress, then these organisms will multiply and be capable of becoming highly pathogenic.

There are many examples of these, ranging from salmonella in calves to swine dysentery and enzootic pneumonia in pigs, and *E. coli* septicaemia in chicken or pasteurella in turkeys. One most successful way of keeping the numbers to a low level is to routinely empty buildings and clean, disinfect, and if necessary fumigate as well. Not only should the buildings be so dealt with, but likewise the surroundings, thereby also eliminating the pests and vermin that can readily carry infection over from one crop to the next. The disinfection process is summarised in Table 3.1.

Table 3.1 The disinfection process in sequence

---

1. Empty the house, and preferably the site, of all livestock.
2. Clean out all 'organic matter' – litter, old feed, any other material that could contain pathogenic micro-organisms. Remove totally from the area of the buildings.
3. Remove all portable equipment for cleaning and disinfecting outside the building.
4. Wash down with heavy-duty detergent-steriliser. Use a power washer wherever possible.
5. Apply a disinfectant appropriate to the type of infections being dealt with. Usually required is a mixture active against viruses, bacteria, parasites and insects which may carry infection from one batch of livestock to another.
6. Wherever possible fumigate with a formaldehyde-active material after the equipment and litter have been reassembled.
7. Dry out and rest for a day or two before restocking.

It may be readily understood that the full process of cleaning and disinfection cannot be achieved unless there are no animals at all in the building, otherwise they would be hurt. If a farmer sees no way of achieving this end because of the size of the building, then it may be worth considering a division of the building into several completely separate sections. It may then be possible to clear sections completely and disinfect them; it is worth emphasising that division of the building will in any case have a merit in reducing the disease challenge and will also almost certainly improve the environmental conditions by keeping the animals in smaller units which may well be better suited to their needs.

Very often there is an expression of scepticism by the stockowner about the value of hygiene and disinfection when it is quite obvious that it will be less than perfect under the conditions of the farm. Re-contamination is always taking place and surfaces cannot be perfectly cleaned. It is, however, better to look at it in a more positive way. Any endeavours that *reduce* the challenge on the animal are likely to be of benefit in one way or another.

Attention should be drawn to the fact that in controlled environment houses with cavities within the structure, especially the insulation of the building, insects may be harboured that can transfer disease from one crop of livestock to another unless they too are destroyed by penetrating fumigation techniques. There are also special dangers of animal accommodation with earth or soil floors. Few disinfectants have very much penetrative power in the presence of soil, though a useful technique is to mix a suitable disinfectant (often a synthetic phenol) with an oil which will soak into the soil, and then cover this with tarred paper or polythene before placing the litter or bedding in position. This will separate the next batch of animals from the contaminated soil for some time, during which there will be continuing action by the disinfectant.

To some extent there is a mistaken belief that disease in the farm animal has been very nearly overcome. This is wrong, since, whilst it is perfectly true that to a large extent the known, recognisable infections have been mastered, a new crop of rather inapparent infections, which are difficult to recognise, have emerged under intensive conditions. The appearance of these infections may show nothing abnormal, apart from poor productivity and conversion efficiency, a lack of uniformity, high rejection rate of carcases, and high mortality. It may only be recognised by a comparison of the results as they are with what they should be. As started earlier, these infections are largely caused by organisms which are normally present in animals and apparently do no harm, but if circumstances are favourable to their multiplication they have serious effects. Thus the attempt is not made to get rid of these organisms, because it would fail, but to reduce their number to a minimum and reduce their unfavourable effects.

The course of events may best be understood by considering some examples in modern animal husbandry. First, consider respiratory disease in the young bovine animal, between the ages of about three months and a year, kept in a covered yard. So far as one can tell, prior to the introduction of modern methods, there were no great problems. Animals were housed at a generous density, ventilation was 'free' through pan-tiled roofs, and a bedding of straw also tended to be generous. Buildings were more often than not narrow, open-fronted and rather like the modern monopitch design which is becoming so popular now. Many of the modern trends have eliminated many of these features. Buildings are wide, totally enclosed, with a metal or asbestos roof which permits no air movement or ventilation. Stocking rates are very high and the amount of bedding used may be minimal or, in those cases where slatted floors are used, is absent altogether. Thus there is great stress on the stock and the debilitating effect of a challenging environment allows certain mixtures of viruses and bacteria, and other pathogens, to come to the fore. This pattern of disease is shown clearly in Table 3.2.

Table 3.2 The disease pattern on the farm

Bad husbandry + Primary disease agent (often a virus)	→	Secondary disease agents (often bacteria or parasites)	→	Clinical or sub-clincal disease

There are certain vaccines available which try to protect the animals from the effect of these organisms, but veterinary surgeons in practice find that the organisms in the vaccine often bear little or no relationship to those that are causing the infection. Vaccines may be a little help on occasion but they can almost never be relied upon. The only true way of dealing with the problem is to get all the husbandry and housing matters right so the animals are not subjected to an excessive challenge.

Another very important example is that of mastitis. Mastitis infection can only actually enter the udder via the orifice at the end of the teat. The chances of mastitis increase considerably if the cows are dirty, if their accommodation promotes the viability of the organisms that can cause disease, and/or if the end of the teat can be injured. In traditional accommodation cows were either kept tied up in a cowshed, which was usually cleaned out daily, or they were given spacious access to a deeply strawed yard. In both cases the animals usually remained fairly clean, but this is far from the case in the highly popular cubicle system of housing cattle. This has a great deal to recommend it in so far as it is low on labour, uses little bedding and a minimum of building space. The trouble is that cubicle beds quite often become dirty at the rear area and there is a tendency for a lot of slurry to accumulate in the passageways so that the cows may become very dirty. That ubiquitous organism, the bacteria *E. coli*, is given favourable conditions to multiply and so *E. coli* mastitis, often called environmental mastitis, has become a major disease in dairy cattle.

Table 3.3 Some examples of bad husbandry with welfare implications

---

1. Overcrowding and too many animals on one site.
2. Mixed ages within a house or site.
3. Excessive movement of animals between pens, houses or sites.
4. Poor ventilation and environmental control.
5. Bad drainage or disposal of dung and bedding.
6. Unhygienic or insufficient food and watering equipment.
7. Absence of good routine disinfection procedures.
8. Faulty nutrition including deficiencies in vitamins and minerals.
9. Feed contaminated with moulds and mycotoxins.
10. Lack of thermal insulation of buildings.
11. Poor control of visitors to prevent disease entry.
12. Absence of protective clothing for all attendants and visitors.
13. Lack of attention to good vaccination and medication procedures.
14. Insufficient reaction to any problems.

Regarding pigs, there are even more examples. Respiratory diseases are a constant problem in the intensively housed animal. The cycle of events often starts with bad ventilation causing invasion of primary virus or mycoplasmal infections of the membranes lining the nose or the lungs. After these have done initial damage, secondary bacteria take over to cause still further injury to the tissue. Thus the complete mechanism here is:

Environmental stress $\longrightarrow$ Invasion by virus or mycoplasma $\longrightarrow$ Secondary bacteria e.g. *Pasteurella Salmonella* or *E. coli.*

The aim in good animal husbandry is to concentrate on the

good measures of husbandry so that the primary challenge never happens.

The scourge of swine dysentery, now a constant problem with intensive pig units, has arisen in parallel with intensivism. What happened was due to the increase in contact between the pigs and their own excreta; underlying influences were the absence of bedding, the use of slatted floors, often of such a design that they were ineffective for self-cleaning and a good deal of muck accumulated between them, and the popularity of 'floor feeding', with the food being tipped over the lying area of the pigs. Often this would be mixed with excreta in varying amounts so the risk of infection was ever present.

Immunity and the young animal

There is a real problem in animal husbandry with the protection of animals from infection during periods when they have poor immunity. When animals are born they have received *in utero*, or in the egg, passive immunity from the dam in relation to the pathogenic organisms, or vaccinal protection experienced by the dam. This passive immunity will, in the case of the mammal, be further fortified by the milk received, and especially that taken by the animal in the first few days of life. This first milk, or colostrum, is very rich in the immuno-globulins or antibodies against local infections. The protection is called 'passive' because it only has a short life, no more than about 3–4 weeks, after which it must be replaced by the 'active' immunity, when the animal produces its own antibodies either through a vaccine or by a natural challenge of the organism. Figure 3.1 shows the general course of events. Now, if the challenge from natural organisms proves to be too great, the animals will become diseased and may succumb.

Before relating how this feature has a bearing on modern husbandry and welfare, it should also be pointed out that the whole immunological system of the animal may be adversely influenced, or even destroyed, by an early infection. The most serious example of this in livestock is Gumboro or infectious bursal disease of poultry, which effectively destroys the immunity of birds for several weeks so that vaccines are of no use and the birds easily and rapidly succumb to every type of infection. Similar events may be recorded in other livestock.

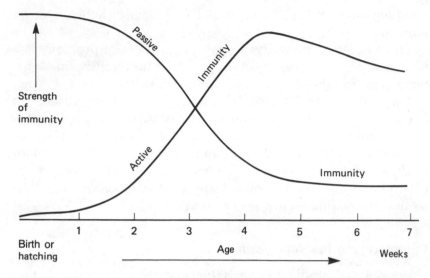

Fig. 3.1 These curves represent antibody levels (i.e. immunity) produced by active or passive immunisation. Animals or birds derive passive immunity from their dams but it is short-lived. Active immunity comes from vaccines but takes time to develop.

Having looked at some of the many ways in which diseases can exert their effect, it is fruitful to see how much better stock will thrive if they are free of disease (SPF or 'specific pathogen-free'). Martineau *et al.* (Table 3.4) collected all the evidence up to 1982 and found there were benefits in growth rate in the order of 10%, and feed conversion efficiency of approximately 9%, together with further benefits in relation to morbidity and mortality.

It is evident from this that welfare will be much better safeguarded if every measure is taken to reduce the incidence and effect of disease.

Table 3.4 Performance traits of 'conventional' and 'SPF' fattening pigs (adapted from Martineau *et al.*, 1982)

	Conventional	SPF
Growth rate (g/day)	603	678
Feed conversion (kg/kg)	3.66	3.05

This table shows the considerable benefits of rearing pigs known to be free of the common pathogens.

How does the young animal's system of passive and active immunity relate to modern intensive husbandry and animal welfare? If a study is made of Fig. 3.1 it will be seen that the passive immunity tends to fall to a 'low' in the order of 3-5 weeks whilst concurrently the active immunity is gradually developing. However, there is an especially vulnerable period which lies in the region of 3-6 weeks when immunity is low, so at this time animals need to be especially protected. Thus from the immunological aspect early weaning of piglets at the age of 3 weeks is a very challenging thing to do and not surprisingly the piglet may easily contract disease at this time. Hence the careful measures taken over housing and management which are given in Chapter 12 are more than justified if weaning must be done at this age for general economic reasons.

There is a further essential which should be emphasised in relation to the development of immunity. Farm animals are certainly growing more quickly due to genetic, nutritional, environmental and health improvements in the past years. As the market and requirements for animals have tended to be for smaller, leaner stock, so the general marketing age is much less than it used to be. This is epitomised particularly in the broiler chicken, which used to take some 13 weeks (90 days) to reach a weight which it currently achieves in well under half that time. If we add to this the fact that breeding stock too on average are younger and are kept a shorter time, then it all adds up to a situation in which the immunological status of the animals on the farm is in a fairly juvenile or underdeveloped stage, which makes it all the more vital to protect the animal from every possible challenge from disease.

This protection is provided in a number of ways, many of which are normal good husbandry and welfare procedures, as can clearly be seen from the following list:

1. Young animals should be placed in accommodation which has been thoroughly cleaned and sterilised.
2. Animals must not be allowed to be contaminated with their own excreta and respirations – good dung disposal and ventilation are essential.
3. Clean bedding will assist in keeping animals clean.
4. Animals should be moved throughout their lifetime as seldom as possible, and particularly during pregnancy, since there is

a danger in the latter case that the young will be born to face a challenge immediately after birth to which they have no immunity at all.

5. Mixing of animals at almost any stage of life is a very dangerous procedure immunologically, and should be avoided wherever possible. In fact many good husbandry systems have developed which involve no move at all, for example, in 'day-old to death' pig pens, and broiler chicken housing. Systems such as this have other advantages and should be pursued more vigorously.

6. There are reasonably well-established norms for maximum numbers of animals in one house or on one site and these should be followed (see Chapter 1). For the same reason recommended figures should be followed to reduce pen size. The sub-division of buildings always helps – and for reasons independent of disease challenge and immunity.

7. Good environmental control maintains animals in a state where they have a maximum ability to resist disease challenges.

8. The use of vaccines and drug administration should be reduced to the minimum. The aim of good husbandry is to assist in building up the animal's natural immunity and it cannot do this if it is overburdened with vaccines and drugs. It has already been stated that no husbandry system should be drug-dependent and if it is it will almost certainly fail, as the organisms become resistant to the drugs. In any case, drug-dependent animals cannot compete with those that are free of infection since a healthy animal will always do better than an animal with pathogenic organisms and drugs – leaving aside of course the cost of the drug, which may be considerable.

Reference

Martineau, G.P., Broes, A., and Martineau-Doize, B. (1982) 'Intérêts et limites de l'assainissement des élevages dans l'économie de la production porcine.' *Ann. Med. Vet.*, **126** 279–313.

4 Climatic Environmental Effects on Welfare

Farm livestock are homeotherms, which means they must maintain their body temperature within quite a narrow range for their comfort, welfare and optimal productivity. In order to achieve this stability the animals maintain a thermal balance between the heat they produce or gain from the environment and the heat they lose to it. In order to appreciate the welfare implications of this it is helpful to consider the routes by which the body loses its heat – these being radiation, convection, conduction and evaporation.

Radiation heat loss arises from the fact that a warm body will emit heat when it is at a temperature higher than that of the surrounding surfaces. The amount of heat loss is affected by the area of the body's surface and the position and behaviour of the animal; for example, heat loss will be greatly reduced when groups of animals are close together. In practice, hot surfaces are to be avoided in summer as they prevent the animal from radiating and thus dissipating surplus heat, while in winter cold surfaces will aggravate heat loss in a cool environment and greatly increase the risk of chilling, especially in the young animal.

Convection loss is governed by the surface area of the animal, its temperature and that of the surrounding air, and the movement of air over the surface. Hence the danger of draughts in cold weather as a source of heat dissipation, in contrast to the need for high air movement in warm weather, which can help to relieve heat stress.

Conduction loss is due to physical contact of the animal with a surface, and is dependent on the temperature of the surface, its area and its thermal conductivity. It is most important to reduce heat loss by conduction, either by providing animals with bedding or by thermally insulating surfaces.

Evaporative heat loss enables an animal to withstand high

temperatures even when the loss by radiation, conduction and convection is insignificant. Evaporation of water from the skin plays a minor role in the thermal balance in farm animals (which for the most part are sparsely equipped with sweat glands) compared to that from the respiratory surfaces. Evaporation from the skin is dependent, so far as external factors are concerned, on the temperature, humidity and movement of the air; from the lungs it depends on the humidity of the inspired and expired air.

Temperature regulation

Farm animals regulate their body temperature in various ways. In hot weather, heat is lost through a higher breathing rate which increases the evaporation of moisture from the lungs, by transudation of moisture through the skin, and through an increased intake of water. Livestock also keep cool by avoiding sunlight, eating less food and reducing movement to a minimum. They are also helped by postural changes: for example, in hot weather the chicken holds its wings out from its body so that the air can circulate over the poorly ventilated underside. Other animals, and principally the pig, wallow to keep cool by evaporation.

In very cold weather farm livestock increase their heat production by eating more. They also increase their insulation against cold by depositing larger amounts of fat under the skin, and by growing longer and coarser hair. Heat production is further increased by shivering, and heat is conserved by huddling to reduce the exposed surface area.

Most of these natural ways of animals adjusting themselves satisfactorily to climatic stress involve a degree of freedom of movement which is absent in many intensive systems.

The effect of humidity

From the aspect of the physiology of the animal, the humidity of the air has a number of very important influences. The amount of water vapour in the air controls the rate of evaporation of moisture from the animal's external surfaces, especially in the lungs and respiratory tract.

In a ventilated building where air currents carry the water

vapour away, continuous evaporation can take place but the degree with which this happens depends on the rate of air movement and the percentage of saturation of the ambient air. Obviously, if the air moving in the building is already saturated, no evaporation can take place.

The term *relative humidity* (RH) refers to the amount of moisture actually in the air compared with the amount it could contain at the same temperature, and is expressed as a percentage. Hence, the amount of moisture in the air at, say, 100% RH will vary, depending on the air temperature.

In practical terms, in temperate climates livestock may thrive perfectly well over a wide range of humidity, probably extending from at least 30 to 90% RH. If, however, ambient temperatures are below the correct level, high humidities will intensify the cold stress, owing to the extra moisture surrounding the animal and being breathed into its lungs. Likewise, at air temperatures above the normally accepted range, a high humidity will progressively reduce the animal's ability to keep cool by evaporation until, if the air is saturated and as warm as the animal, it will lose this ability altogether. A very dry air, below about 30% RH, may dehydrate the mucous membranes of the respiratory tract and make them more vulnerable to invasion by pathogenic organisms, and create discomfort and a dry and scurfy skin. There will also be direct effects on the viability of pathogenic organisms, which is referred to in Chapter 5. It is our constant aim in livestock buildings so to ventilate them that the moisture produced by the animals is liberated from the atmosphere.

Air movement

At air temperatures above the body temperature, air movement tends to reduce heat dissipation by increasing the flow of heat from the environment through the skin into the body of the animal. The air movement in fact reduces the insulation of the surrounding air and may also reduce that of the hair and feathers themselves. At cold temperatures, on the other hand, excessive air movement in the form of a draught may chill an animal which would otherwise be quite comfortable, and much attention is rightly given to this factor in practice. In subsequent sections dealing with individual species, a range of acceptable air movements will be given.

The effect of the animal's surface

Although the sweating mechanism of most farm animals is poor, water vapour is still passed through the skin by 'insensible perspiration'. The exchange of heat through the body is also affected by the colour of the skin, its physical nature and its disposition in relation to the environment and thereby the risk of a serious welfare problem is minimised.

The amount of solar radiation absorbed by the coat is determined to some extent by its colour. A white coat may absorb only 20% of the visible radiation falling on it; a black coat almost 100%. Half the energy in the solar spectrum is the invisible infra-red portion, which can be completely absorbed on the coat.

The colour of the skin itself is also important in its reaction to sunburn and photosensitisation. A white coat with a smooth and glossy texture minimises the adverse effects of direct sunlight. Shade reduces the great heat load which may fall on animals. The coat also influences convective and evaporative loss from the skin. If it is thick and/or long, it will entrap air and moisture and slow down the convection exchange. It also provides a local climate of high humidity and so renders the exchange of heat by vaporisation of water from the skin surface more difficult.

Environment zones for livestock

It is apparent that there is no absolute temperature at which animals must be maintained; every animal, and even more so every group of animals, has a range within which it can give optimal performance. The range within which one would like to keep all animals is the 'thermocomfort' zone. Within this range animals are not merely capable of giving an optimal perform-ance, they also feel such comfort that they have no preference for any particular location – neither huddling nor separating, to keep warm or cool, respectively. They are, as it were, in complete harmony with their environment.

The range is difficult to define absolutely because its precise nature will depend on many factors, such as age, weight, feeding level, past experience (acclimatisation) and husbandry system. It may be a very narrow zone, as for the day-old chick or piglet, or a very wide zone, as for adult cattle. It is rarely economic to keep animals within the thermocomfort zone at all times, although we may aim for it in our building designs.

Outside this zone, both higher and lower, is the temperature zone known as the 'thermoneutral' zone, and it is vital to try and maintain stock within this all the time if they are housed, and at least most of the time if they are outdoors. It is the zone in which no metabolic demands are made on the animals. They maintain homeothermy by quite extensive fluctuations in their behaviour (postural changes, huddling, etc.), by changes in their hair disposition (piloerection in the cold) or blood circulation at the surface, and by perspiration and panting. They can do all these without any measurable metabolic changes, so that productivity can go apace although, because the animals may behave differently in response to the changes, there may be problems with vices and/or environmental pollution if there is an excessive favouring of certain parts of a pen or building.

If the temperature falls below the lower end of the scale (the lower critical temperature), the animal will need to use more food to keep warm, so that it either produces less if it is on a fixed feeding scale, or eats more to keep warm and still produce at an optimal level. If the animal is largely a roughage consumer, such as adult cattle or sheep, this may matter very little, because the food will be relatively cheap, but if it is a consumer of expensive concentrates, it is a very uneconomic way to keep the animal warm. This is an important reason why non-ruminant livestock, such as pigs and poultry, are kept in well-insulated housing with controlled ventilation, whereas the ruminants are not provided with such sophistication.

If the temperature goes above the top of the thermoneutral zone, the animal must try and reduce its heat production and it will tend to do this by lowering its food consumption and productivity.

If temperatures continue to go upwards or downwards, above or below the upper or lower critical temperatures respectively, the animal continues to try and maintain its homeothermy by various metabolic means, but in due course the deep body temperature is altered and it will, at extremes, eventually collapse and die. Fortunately, in livestock housing we do not often have to face such excessive problems, but even in temperate climates they can arise owing to bad design or failure of the environmental control system. The ambient temperatures

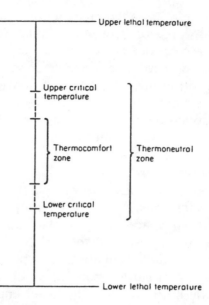

Fig. 4.1 Environment zones for livestock

at which animals succumb are known as the lethal temperatures, there being one at the top and one at the bottom end of the scale (Fig. 4.1).

Cattle

In most cool, temperate environments, ruminants maintain homeothermy by regulating evaporative loss at little metabolic cost in order to keep cool. Moreover, ruminants have a very marked ability to alter their zone of thermal neutrality in response to previous thermal history. There are thus no absolute criteria for the thermal requirements of any class of ruminant livestock, except perhaps the newborn animal; they depend to a very large extent on what the animal has grown accustomed to.

Thermal requirements

In an unheated building at low air movement the only cattle likely to experience cold sufficient to elevate the heat production are newborn calves, or young calves whose metabolic rate is low by virtue of starvation, or sickness, or emaciation. Such animals can undoubtedly be stressed by cold in unheated buildings and may require special attention. The most practical, immediate, and cheap answer is to provide a warm 'kennel' with straw bale walls and a straw roof.

Within a few weeks of birth the healthy calf with a good appetite has a critical temperature close to 0°C and is not likely to be stressed by cold while indoors. Well grown veal calves, by virtue of their very high energy intake and heat production, are particularly tolerant to cold and, by the same criteria, sensitive to heat. The traditional belief that veal calves should be kept in a warm environment because they are not ruminant and are therefore somehow more sensitive to cold is unscientific and untrue. As explained in a later chapter, very satisfactory conditions can be provided for veal calves in open-fronted deep-straw yards.

No other class of cattle is likely to experience a systemic stress of cold when standing up in a dry enclosure unless air movement is exceptionally high. For the dairy cow, however, cold stress should not be considered as a systemic but as a local problem. Heat production in the high yielding cow is again very high and so the critical temperature is low. Milk synthesis, however, depends on blood flow to the mammary gland, which is reduced by local cooling. The production of dairy cows has been shown to fall at temperatures below about 0°C, although direct chilling of the udder depends as much on the thermal quality of the floor as on the temperature.

It is worthy of stress that European cattle tend to be tolerant to cold but intolerant to heat. Their 'comfort zone' is between about 0 and 20°C. The effect of high temperatures may be ameliorated in practice in a number of ways. The provision of shade makes a great difference, as do wallows and artificial showers.

In loose housing systems with open-fronted barns, protection from solar radiation and maximum provision of air movement represent the limit of environmental improvement. With closed buildings, such as the cowhouse, air conditioning may have to be used and, in parts of the world where climatic temperatures warrant it, it has been found worthwhile.

To summarise, there is no class of healthy ruminant for which the direct effects of low air temperature *per se* are likely to cause intolerable stress in the temperate and cool zones of the world. Moreover, the effects of air temperature below the critical temperature on food conversion efficiency are likely to affect only the smallest animals, at a time when their daily intake is very small relative to lifetime requirements. Thus there are no sound economic grounds for providing any more environmental control for the healthy ruminant animal than shelter from excessive air movement and precipitation.

Pigs

The young piglet is very poorly endowed with hair or subcutaneous fat and has a thick skin. Losses in piglets are relatively high, generally running at about 10–15% before weaning. Many losses are due to chilling and crushing, both factors that can be dealt with by good environmental control and housing. The vast majority of the losses due to poor environmental control occur in the first few days of life; thereafter the effects of poor environment are to cause not so much mortality and disease as a loss in productivity, in respect of both liveweight gain and food conversion efficiency. By adulthood pigs have become reasonably adaptable to a wide range of conditions which are not markedly different from those of other farm livestock.

Piglets

Newly born piglets have a poorly developed heat regulating ability, although their homeothermic mechanisms develop quickly. During the first few hours after birth the body temperature depression under cool housing conditions may be as much as 7°C though the average under satisfactory conditions will be approximately 2°C. The heavier piglet is able to withstand climatic changes better than the small piglet. It is also much more able to resist crushing and there is significant correlation between the weight of a pig and its ability to withstand cold stress. This emphasises the importance of the management of the sow in pregnancy in influencing the viability of the piglet subsequently born to it.

As to the heat loss, evaporative heat loss accounts for only about 10%. The partitioning of the remaining 90% is dependent on the floor. On concrete, about 15% of heat loss is to the floor, 40% by radiation and 35% by convection. On wood, only 6% is

Temperature	Air movement below 0.15 m/sec	Air movement from 0.15-0.25 m/sec	Air movement from 0.25-0.38 m/sec
21°C	Pigs of all ages comfortable	Pigs of all ages comfortable	Young piglets uncomfortable (1-8 weeks)
18°C	Pigs below 1 week uncomfortable	Pigs below 5 weeks uncomfortable	Pigs below 12 weeks uncomfortable
15°C	Pigs below 10 days uncomfortable	Young piglets (c.1-3 weeks old) uncomfortable	Pigs below 12 weeks uncomfortable
13°C	Pigs below 8 weeks uncomfortable	Pigs below 12 weeks uncomfortable	Pigs below 14 weeks uncomfortable
10°C	Pigs below 15 weeks uncomfortable	Pigs below c.16 weeks uncomfortable	Pigs below 16 weeks uncomfortable
7°C	Pigs below 20 weeks uncomfortable	Pigs below 14 weeks uncomfortable	Pigs below 20 weeks uncomfortable
4°C	Pigs below 20 weeks uncomfortable	Pigs below 20 weeks uncomfortable	Pigs below 20 weeks uncomfortable
2°C	All fattening pigs uncomfortable		

Fig 4.2 Chart showing the combined effect of ambient temperature and air movement on the comfort of pigs

to the floor, and on polystyrene a mere 2%. Substituting 12 mm of wood for 25 mm of concrete is equivalent to raising the floor temperature by 12°C. Raising the air speed from 0.1 to 0.3 m/s is equivalent to lowering the air temperature by 13°C.

These findings agree with the observations made by the author regarding the comfort level of piglets and given in Fig. 4.2, which show that by doubling air velocities the air temperature requirements rise by 12°C. All these facts empha-sise the need for straw, shavings or other bedding to be placed over the concrete on the floor, and the necessity for warmth and freedom from high air movement. With these exacting provisions successfully achieved the piglets are encouraged to lie away from the sow and the danger of crushing is greatly reduced.

Growers and fatteners

The daily gain appears to reach a maximum at about 23°C for 40 kg pigs, reducing to approximately 15°C at 90 kg (bacon weight). It has also been found that at the temperature at which the maximum weight gain took place, the food was converted at its maximum efficiency.

Although this data is reliable, there are a number of conflicting reports which suggest that the range in practice may be wider than indicated above. For example, animals penned in groups, as opposed to being penned separately, can thrive at lower house temperatures owing to the effects of huddling and the reduction of radiation loss.

Temperature *per se* is not a good indicator of the environmental requirements for keeping fattening pigs any more than it is for piglets, and full consideration must also be given to air movement, humidity and radiation from surrounding surfaces.

Summarising, it would seem that while the temperature requirements of the grower are well defined for the individually housed pig without bedding, a wider tolerance is acceptable in practice, where acclimatisation, grouping effects and bedding can alter the picture considerably. Nevertheless the limits are reasonably well defined for temperature, but this is not the case with air movement and humidity, on which much less work has been done. The effects of humidity appear to be associated more with an indirect one of disease, but a more accurate definition of these effects is needed.

Breeding pigs

Most of the investigation done on sows has been concerned with the ill-effects of high temperatures. Even though sows exposed to temperatures as high as 37°C for periods of about 8 days could still generally produce normal litters, it seemed however that in-pig sows showed more stress than empty ones owing to the increased metabolic load. The best temperature for the sow is not the best for the piglet, the litter thriving best at 27°C and the sow at approximately 16°C. Where temperatures habitually stay above 29°C it is clear that there is justification for the provision of cooling devices such as sprinklers, sprays and wallows, in addition to shade. Many reports from warm areas of the world confirm this.

Much work remains to be done on the climatic needs of the breeding pig. For example, the special needs of the pregnant sow under the less generous rationing systems now advised, or the relatively immobile conditions of the sow stall. It is reasonable to assume that such animals would require higher temperatures than those kept, for example, in deeply strawed yards or kennels under traditional feeding programmes. There is also no clear definition of the first few days after farrowing, when it is known that the sow's metabolic rate is much reduced and therefore its susceptibility to chilling may be increased.

Stocking density

It is important to stock a piggery to its *optimal* capacity; a full pen of pigs is usually the cleanest and most comfortable group. However, the *optimal* figure does not mean 'packing in' the pigs too tightly or there will be significantly harmful effects on growth, food conversion efficiency and the incidence of disease, and very frequently an increase in the incidence of injury and vice.

Results of extensive trials (Sainsbury, 1978) have shown the following with pigs stocked at 0.46, 0.92 and 1.8 m^2 per head:

m^2/pig	Gain in wt. during experiment (kg)	Average daily feed (kg)	Feed/unit gain (kg)
0.46	40.4	2.40	4.09
0.92	42.0	2.37	3.86
1.80	45.0	2.36	3.69

These show strikingly the bad effect of over-stocking.

Investigations on the effect of numbers of pigs per pen have showed the following:

No. of pigs/pen	Gain (kg)	Average daily gain (kg)	Feed/unit gain (kg)
3	42.7	2.56	3.15
6	42.5	2.32	3.71
12	42.2	2.26	3.79

It is apparent from this work that fatteners benefit quite markedly from plenty of space and small pen size.

Similar results over a tighter range of stocking rates are shown in Table 4.1, summarising work by Hanrahan (1982). This shows that even a relatively modest increase in stocking density has an adverse effect on weight gain and feed conversion efficiency, also with some significant sex differences.

Table 4.1   Effect of stocking rate (SR) and sex on pig performance (from Hanrahan, 1982)

| | Stocking rate (m^2/pig) | | | | | |
| | 0.64 | | 0.57 | | Significance | |
	Male	Female	Male	Female	SR	Sex
No. of pigs	320	320	360	360		
Initial weight	32.5	32.5	31.5	32.2		
Final weight	83.5	83.2	83.3	83.2		
Feed intake/day	2.13	2.16	2.08	2.09	**	ns
Gain/day (g)	716	656	680	617	***	***
Feed/kg gain (kg)	2.99	3.30	3.06	3.40	*	***

ns = no significance * = slightly significant ** = significant *** = highly significant

The harmful effects of heavy stocking seem sufficiently pronounced at least to be noted carefully by the designer and farmer. About 12–20 pigs per pen is probably the ideal number and is unlikely ever to be an unwise or an uneconomic choice; extremely dense stocking may, however, retard the growth of pigs unless the environmental conditions are carefully maintained at the optimum.

Poultry

The most widely used method of brooding chicks is to arrange a source of warmth in a limited area of a house of about 35°C (95°F) at day-old and then subsequently reduce this by 3°C (5°F) per week.

Brooding systems with fairly large warmed areas have considerable merit. They enable a wider distribution of birds in environmentally suitable areas with more space available, factors which are known to improve growth and reduce the likelihood of disease. To ensure a good use of the house, the ambient temperature is at least as important as the brooder temperature, a range of 25–30°C (75–85°F) being associated with the best all-round performance. Below and above this range, weight gains and food conversion efficiencies are reduced. The best performance will probably be obtained if the house temperature is reduced from 30°C (86°F) during the first week to 27°C (81°F) in the second, and 24°C (65°F) in the third.

The worst results are associated with correct brooder temperatures and low house temperatures, below 20°C (68°F), when the chicks are reluctant to venture away from the heat to find food and water. On the other hand, too high a house temperature restricts appetite and retards activity and growth. If the chicks are to be well distributed within the brooding area the temperature must be uniform and draughts at floor level avoided. Overhead, largely radiant sources of heat give the most satisfactory results since their fine thermostatic control and adjustable height offer flexible arrangements. They also serve the dual purpose of brooding and space heating.

Post-brooding temperatures

From the age of three weeks onwards some further reductions in temperature are justified. In the case of broilers, the house temperature should be in the range of 18–21°C (65–70°F) with a definite tendency to the upper figure if there is any danger of the temperature dropping below 18°C (65°F) owing to external conditions. A reduction of some 6°C (11°F) between three to nine weeks, giving an eventual temperature of 13–16°C (55–60°F), is desirable for optimum growth. These temperatures tend to be somewhat lower than those in common practice but their maintenance has important repercussions in reducing heating and ventilation costs and cutting down the effect and incidence of respiratory disease. Obviously low temperatures cannot be maintained in summer but this is compensated for to some extent by increasing the ventilation and air velocity, if the fans have the capacity to achieve it.

Temperature for layers

For intensively kept birds, the optimal temperature is high, that is, about 21°C (70°F). At temperatures below this there is a depression of about ½ egg per hen housed per year per 0.5°C (1°F). Feed intake will be reduced by about 7 g per bird per day for a rise of from 15° to 21°C (60 to 70°F). On the debit side, there is some depression in egg weight, estimated to be about 1 g per egg per 3°C (6°F) rise over 15°C (60°F), but this is far outweighed by the benefits and it is estimated that if a house is kept at 21°C (70°F) rather than 15°C (60°F), then the potential saving in terms of profit margins could be as much as a 20–30% increase in profit.

It should be emphasised that the hen is reasonably adaptable and tolerant to environmental changes and there is a wide range within which it can produce economically even if not at an optimal rate. This range is about 5–24°C (40–75°F). However, this does not mean that the temperature can swing rapidly between these two extremes, since rapid changes of any sort are undesirable. Rather, it represents the seasonal extremes one should aim for at the outside in designing the housing in the case of less intensive systems than the battery, such as deep-litter and the straw yard. Provided the changes take place gradually, birds can acclimatise themselves to them. For short-term variation, as between day and night, a maximum of 6°C (11°F) is a good aim.

If the temperature rises above 24°C (75°F) for lengthy periods the total number of eggs laid and their weight and quality will certainly suffer. Appetite will also fall. Below 5°C (40°F) the chief effect will be a sharply rising appetite, though egg weight and quality can benefit slightly. Figure 4.3 shows the essential features of a well-designed, naturally ventilated poultry house for hot climates.

Water cooling

Welfare problems quite frequently occur in temperate climates, and often in hot climates, with buildings becoming overheated, sometimes for quite long periods. This may sometimes arise from poor thermal insulation of the building, or there may be insufficient ventilation or fans or they may be operating inefficiently. If these obvious faults cannot be corrected, or in

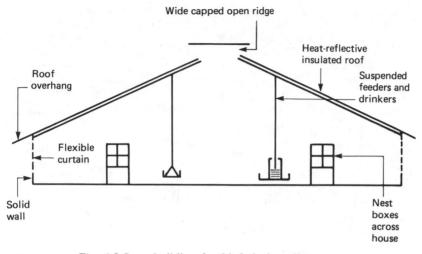

Fig. 4.3 Span building for birds in hot climates

cases where after this it is still too warm, there are several ways of using water to cool the building.

A simple device is to spray water over the roof and walls, thereby cooling by evaporation; in some cases a perforated waterpipe is placed along the roof ridge to discharge water uniformly along the length of the roof. A more usual way is to pass the incoming air through wet pads; the pads may consist of a wooden frame filled with absorbent wood fibres with water falling through from top to bottom. Surplus water has to be collected and recirculated to be economical and the pads must be kept clean if they are to function successfully.

An even better way is to have spray nozzles which produce a very fine mist. They do, however, need a pump and run-off for surplus water.

A fourth method, and perhaps the best of all, consists of a metal disc revolving at high speed which throws off water onto an atomising plate which sets up a very fine mist taken up by the air stream. Good control is achievable by a solenoid valve activated by a humidistat (Fig. 4.4).

Lighting requirements

In nature, the development of the reproductive (egg-laying) organ is stimulated by increasing amounts of daylight, as in

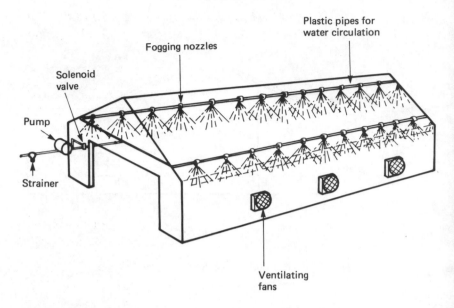

Fig. 4.4 Illustration of a high-pressure misting (fogging) evaporative cooling system in a poultry house

spring, but is depressed when this is reduced, as in autumn. The modern genetically improved layer, under the stimulus of spring-like conditions, will lay before sufficient bodily development has taken place to fully support egg production and it will not be able to lay either the number of eggs or the larger sizes of which it would later be capable. An autumn-like pattern, or even a constant day length, before the bird starts laying, will allow the body to develop properly. Thereafter, to stimulate maximum production, the procedure is to give a weekly increase of light duration of about 20 minutes up to a maximum of 16 to 18 hours. Some form of artificial lighting is of course essential if this is to be achieved in all seasons, though by rearing chicks in the autumn, good use can be made of the natural advantage of seasonal changes.

Clearly, it is to the benefit of the bird's welfare to provide it with a lighting pattern that reduces the likelihood of 'precocious' egg laying. If egg laying starts too early there may well be a higher incidence of egg peritonitis and prolapse, with the inevitable suffering in those birds affected.

There are a number of techniques used in order to get the most favourable response. Each breeder tends to suggest something different for his own stock, based on sound practical experience. A programme is given below for a well-known commercial hybrid.

0–1 week	18 hours light, 6 hours darkness.
2–18 weeks	6 hours light, 18 hours darkness.
19–22 weeks	Increase light by 45 minutes per week to give a good stimulus at the first period of laying.
23–49 weeks	Increase light by 20 minutes per week.
49 weeks onwards	The lighting is kept steady at 18 hours light per day.

For broilers the usual pattern throughout most of the industry is to have 23 hours lighting and 1 hour darkness in each 24 hours, the latter being necessary to train the birds to darkness. If this is not done and the light is suddenly withdrawn for some reason, a pile-up is a likely consequence, the birds tending to crowd into corners and suffocate.

Continous lighting for broilers can be provided with a light intensity as low as 0.2 lux, which is about as low as the 'off' phase in a controlled environment house in the daytime. However, it must be emphasised that provision must be made for adequate artificial lighting at all times when inspection is needed. It is desirable that lighting circuits are provided with dimming systems so that regulation of intensity can be instantaneous.

References

Hanrahan, T.J. (1982) 'Observations of the effects of stocking rate on the performance of gilts and boars to bacon weight' in *The Welfare of Pigs* pp. 141–147. The Hague: Martinus Nijhoff.

Sainsbury, D. (1978) Quoted on p. 41 in *Pig Housing*. Ipswich: Farming Press Ltd.

5 Environmental Factors Affecting Susceptibility to Disease

Animals normally live in harmony with many potentially pathogenic micro-organisms: the major enteric and respiratory diseases are associated with a multiplicity of agents and it is extremely difficult to reproduce clinical disease by experimental infections even when huge doses of these organisms are administered. Whether or not an animal becomes clinically affected depends on a possible host of non-specific factors such as climate, housing and husbandry which together form the total environment which is considered in this book. It should again be made clear that the state of health of the animals can transcend all other factors in determining the economic viability and probable welfare of a livestock enterprise. Disease at its worst kills the animal, but even in sub-lethal infections seriously affects productivity.

Droplet infections are the main mode of spread of a variety of contagious diseases and many pathogens have been shown to have spread in this way, via the breath and also from secretions and excretions of the infected animals. The environmental conditions in the houses also have their effects on the viability of the pathogens.

Referring specifically to virus particles, a general trend is that high ambient temperatures are more harmful to their survival than low ones. The effect of relative humidity on viruses in general is that some viruses survive best at a low relative humidity, whereas others survive best at a high relative humidity.

So far as bacteria are concerned, a rise in temperature causes their increasing destruction, but airborne spores are highly resistant. The universal potential pathogen *E. coli* survives and multiplies best at about 15°C, as also do *Mycoplasms*. Bacteria tend to be resistant to low and high RH but sensitive to mid-range RH, but bacterial spores are almost totally resistant to RH effects.

It is important to be aware that with airborne infections the size of the infecting dose will determine whether or not disease will result, and also, its severity and the likelihood of infection making headway will depend on the animal's overall resistance; for example, chilling can markedly lower an animal's resistance to inhaled pathogens.

At the present time, ventilation systems in which the air is recirculated are being favoured by designers as a means of reducing heating costs but this approach is very dangerous and in such systems some form of air cleansing, such as filtration, may be essential to avoid a build-up of pathogens. Such dangers have been very well illustrated in the human field in outbreaks of 'Legionnaire's Disease' after contamination by the bacterial agent in hospitals' air circulation systems.

The disposal of large accumulations of animal excrement, bedding and litter is a further problem and can, in some instances, be the limiting factor in determining the size of unit. It is common practice to dilute the effluent from farm buildings into a slurry and then spray it over farmland as a fertiliser. The hazard from the dissemination of slurry-associated pathogens over a wide area in this way can be considerable, particularly in windy weather. A dairy herd of 50 cows plus 50 sows and their litters cause a potential pollution load as large as that of a village of 1 000 people, yet frequently the manure is carelessly disposed of without thought of its potential dangers and hazards to man or animal.

There is considerable evidence to show how methods of housing influence injury and disease and some examples are given in Tables 5.1–5.6

In a survey by Hannan and Murphy (Table 5.1), a widespread examination was carried out of cattle kept completely on slats, which are a considerable welfare risk, and on straw, which is looked upon as the desirable bedding for housed cattle. Their survey, covering some 15 000 cattle, showed a disease incidence twice as great on slats as on straw, which was highly significant statistically. Only clinical parasitism had a higher incidence on straw than on slats.

From the welfare aspect possibly the greatest risk is injury causing lameness, and the authors of this survey comment that lameness cases 'were more severe or extensive in cattle on slats'. Continuing with problems arising from slats, Ekesbo (1983)

Table 5.1 Disease incidence in bullocks kept on slats and on straw, expressed as percentage of cattle at risk (from a survey by Hannan and Murphy, 1983)

Disease category	Slatted floors, 12 010 cattle at risk	Straw yards, 2 882 cattle at risk	Significance of difference
Lameness	4.75	2.43	P<0.001
Eye disease	2.09	0.97	P<0.001
Skin disease	0.91	0.07	P<0.001
Acute ruminal impactions	0.38	0.17	ns
Injury	0.30	0.24	ns
Abscessations	0.27	0.10	ns
Clinical parasitism	0.25	0.80	−P<0.001
Enteritis	0.23	0.00	P<0.05
Respiratory disease	0.16	0.10	ns
Other diseases	0.39	0.54	ns
All diseases	9.73	5.42	P<0.001

It can be seen that whilst lameness was the most common disease observed in both husbandry systems the incidence was twice as great on slatted floors. In addition, cases were more severe or extensive in those cattle on slats. Eye and skin diseases were also significantly more prevalent than in straw yards. The overall incidence of disease was almost twice as great in slatted floor houses.

quotes the work of Bäckström with pigs, showing further harmful effects in a different species. Sows had twice as many foot lesions in pens with *partly* slatted floors, whilst piglets also showed significantly higher rates of mortality, enteritis and unthriftiness in pens with partly slatted floors (Table 5.2 and 5.3).

The author ascribes many of the problems of the increased ill-health of pigs on slats to the toxic gases that can emerge from the slurry underneath.

In the cases of pigs in pens without slats, the benefit was predominant apparently because the animals were provided with solid beds and with some straw bedding, but it has been shown that just providing straw *to eat* in the case of pigs has benefits. The work of Jongebreur (Table 5.4) shows strikingly that even a

Table 5.2 Number of sows during gestation and lactation and incidence of sow foot lesions in pens with and without partly slatted floors (from Bäckström, 1973: quoted by Ekesbo, 1982)

	Without slats	Partly slatted	Statistical difference
Number of sows	3 500	588	***
Foot lesions (%)	3.3	6.3	***

Table 5.3 Number of litters, number of piglets born piglet mortality and litter morbidity in pens with crates with and without partly slatted floors (from Bäckström, 1973: quoted by Ekesbo, 1982)

	Pen floor		Statistical difference
	Without slats	Partly slatted	
No. of litters	1 393	681	
No. of piglets born	15 902	7 906	
Total mortality (%)	9.0	11.9	***
Diarrhoea (%)	10.8	17.6	***
'Unthrifty' (%)	18.3	26.0	***
Total morbidity (%)	57.2	62.8	*

Tables 5.2 and 5.3 show clearly the advantages to pigs of solid floors compared with slatted floors.

Table 5.4 The effects of the supply of straw on the number of injured tails (from Jongebreur, 1983)

	Straw	No straw
No. of animals	6 661	6 387
No. of farms	4	4
No. of injured tails	125	245
Quantity of straw/pig (g) on the different farms	350–880	0

modest amount of straw, in this case provided in a box which the pigs could eat whilst housed on fully slatted floors, greatly reduced the number of injured (cannibalised) tails. The straw produced this beneficial effect by (a) providing pigs with

Table 5.5 Relative frequencies of some behavioural patterns of importance to animal welfare in different housing systems for weaned piglets (from Jongebreur, 1983)

Behaviour	Open barn with straw	Flat-deck cage
Rooting on objects	100	38
Rooting on pigs	100	467
Massaging pigs	100	195
Nibbling at pigs	100	700

Table 5.6 Performance and health of veal calves in crates and straw yards (from Webster and Saville, 1981)

	Crated calves bucket-fed	Straw yard calves teat-fed	
	Friesian bulls	Friesian bulls	Hereford x Friesian heifers
Finish weight (kg)	203	172	161
Days on feed	112	96	98
Killing-out (%)	58	56	57
Milk consumption (kg)	226	210	203
Food conversion ratio	1.46	1.69	1.69
Deaths and culls	11	8	8
Treatment courses (%)			
Respiratory disease	5	42	22
Enteric disease	25	25	12

The data in this table shows that whilst results in the calves reared on straw are not quite as good as those kept in crates, the 'alternative', system is, and indeed certainly has been found to be, commercially viable.

However, as with all loose-housed systems, it is necessary for the management to be superior if results are to be as satisfactory as those for individually managed systems.

something to do and (b) probably providing a diet which was more balanced, fibrous and 'comfortable'. This is further shown in Jongebreur's work (op. cit.) (Table 5.5) illustrating aberrant behaviour of pigs kept without straw, where there is much greater rooting and massaging of each other and above seven times as great an incidence of nibbling, which can eventually lead to cannibalism. It should never be forgotten that before pigs were kept on slatted floors and/or without bedding, tail-biting and other forms of cannibalism were virtually unknown. One must nevertheless beware of believing that it is only by returning to 'old' methods that everything will be all right.

A comparative trial by Webster and Saville showed that calves in straw yards failed to do as well as those in crates on wooden slatted floors (Table 5.6). Nevertheless the difference was not great and the inference may be that management changes might succeed in improving the situation.

References

Ekesbo, I. (1982) 'Some aspects of sow health and housing.' in *The Welfare of Pigs* pp. 250–263. The Hague: Martinus Nijhoff.

Hannan, J. and Murphy, P. (1983) 'Comparative mortality and morbidity rates for cattle on slatted floors.' in *Indicators Relevant to Farm Animal Welfare* pp. 139–142. The Hague: Martinus Nijhoff.

Jongebreur, A.A. (1983) 'Housing design and welfare in livestock production.' in *Farm Animal Housing and Welfare* pp. 265–269. The Hague: Martinus Nijhoff.

Webster, A.J.F. and Saville, C. (1981) 'Rearing of veal calves.' in *Alternatives to Intensive Husbandry Systems* p. 86. London: UFAW.

6 Thermal Comfort and Thermal Insulation

Most farm animals in this country in the rearing stage or when they are being fattened, and in some cases even in the adult stage, require warmth which is well above the ambient through much of the year. Warm equable temperatures are necessary for optimal productivity but they also have other functions in maintaining the comfort of the animals. Warmth may be provided by applying artificial heating but this is too expensive a procedure unless it is absolutely necessary and so the key to a good animal house is a high standard of thermal insulation to conserve heat. This is its main function, and of course it is just as important in reducing heat loss if artificial heating is applied, but there are many vital extra advantages of thermal insulation.

It is a principal method of preventing condensation; condensation exacerbates cold and aggravates the deleterious effects, quite apart from the damage that may be done to the structure of a house when condensation takes place. Bedding becomes damp and usage will be increased. Thermal insulation helps to prevent diurnal variations in conditions and will help to keep the building cooler in the summer. Moreover, it is a great aid to good ventilation, especially natural ventilation, since warm air keeps flowing upwards to extracting points when the surfaces are warm, whereas if these are cold the air may recirculate within the building. When animals are actually in contact with the surface, lying on the floor when there is no bedding, it can readily be understood that a warm surface is vital for the comfort of the animal and the prevention of heat loss.

Methods of insulation vary enormously but basically there are two systems that may be used – the permanent and hygienic, or the temporary and disposable.

The 'permanent and hygienic' method is usually a part of the building structure itself, with insulation linings to the roof and walls and an insulated structure somewhere in the construction of the floor. It is quite a complicated affair to achieve satisfactory construction in an animal house. Apart from the demands for a really high standard of insulation it is also necessary to ensure a smooth and hygienic inner surface that does not interrupt air flow and can be easily kept clean. Furthermore, and of extreme importance, so far as possible the insulation itself must be kept free of vermin and insects. Apart from the fact that they can easily destroy the insulation materials, they are also capable of carrying most pathogenic organisms. When a house is emptied of livestock they tend to retreat into the insulation of the building, if they can, where they may be protected from the cleaning process. Hence the construction must do what it can to guard against this.

The insulation also has to be adequately protected from moisture penetration, not so much in terms of weatherproofing, though that is obviously important, but rather more from water vapour from within the building which will tend to seep into the construction, if there is no seal, and condense at some point where it meets its dew point. The result is quite disastrous: the insulation is largely lost, the construction gets wet and deteriorates, and drips of moisture are likely on the floor, the bedding and the animals. The damp atmosphere, if the temperature is also cold, will create a physiological stress on the animals whilst it is also likely to be most favourable for the viability of the pathogenic organisms.

There is a multitude of ways of achieving good insulation, but whichever is used the criteria mentioned must not be flouted.

Temporary and disposable insulation is also as important and as valuable in its way. It may be that the building seems too cold and damp and a cheap and easy way must be sought to protect the animals. The answer is usually straw – and plenty of it – fixed over the animals, often suspended by wire, and protected from damp penetration from within the building by polythene sheets or any other suitable vapourproof material – plastic fertiliser bags are a favourite because they are usually around and can be well-lagged at the joints to do quite a satisfactory job.

Another approach is not to try and insulate the whole roof or building but just a local area where the animals lie, making a roofed kennel with straw. I would guess that as many animals have found comfort and welfare from this simple process as

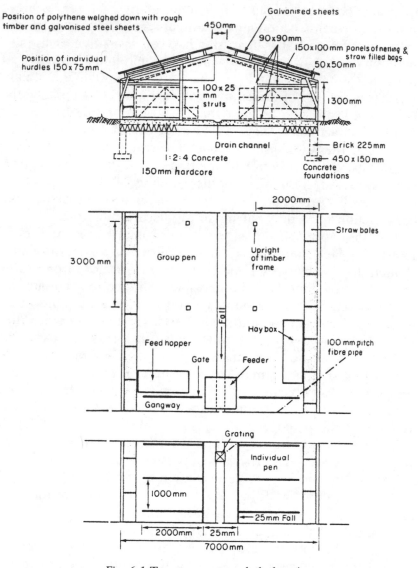

Fig. 6.1 Temporary straw-bale housing

from dozens of man's other, more sophisticated attempts. So successful is this use of temporary straw insualtion that it can lead to one mistake, and that is, to leave the temporary cover in position for too long. It can then be a great danger, constituting a risk as harbourer of vermin and of pathogens.

Some mention may also be made of the merits of the

temporary house for animals. There are many reasons why temporary housing is needed – perhaps urgently. For example, it may be necessary to keep animals longer than expected due to changing market requirements, or it may be that almost instant isolation housing is needed. To relieve the tension on a building or on space is one of the best ways of preventing problems developing or assuaging those that have.

A traditional way of providing this sort of accommodation is with straw-baled walls and corrugated iron roof sheets (Fig. 6.1). Provided these two basic materials are available, not much more is needed to get the building done. Such a house may be a little difficult to manage but will probably give superb results for a year, after which it should be destroyed.

More recently there has emerged a vogue for temporary buildings of polythene on semi-circular frames. These can form a very useful way of providing temporary housing to cope with the emergency, and provide for the good welfare of the stock. A virtue of these forms of housing, whichever is favoured, is that they are usually cheap enough to allow the farmer to house the stock, providing them with very generous space allowances which will have all-round beneficial effects. A danger is that they will be used permanently!

7 Natural Ventilation and Lighting

Natural ventilation may appear at first sight to be a thoroughly uncertain system that will depend far too much on the whims of the weather to be successful in modern animal production, but this is really not the case at all. It can be carefully planned just like mechanical ventilation and can serve the livestock as adequately if this is done. Also, it has the great advantage that there is very little to go wrong with this system and the concern over breakdown, which certainly dominates our planning of the mechanical system, is removed. In principle it depends on three 'forces' for its satisfactory working: the 'stack effect', 'aspiration', and 'perflation'. The 'stack effect' is the ventilation due to the rising of warm, stale air which is lighter, to be replaced by cooler fresh air from outside the building. It is the principal motivating force in cool and temperate weather. 'Aspiration' is the sucking out of the air from a building when the wind blows over it, the air being drawn out from ridge openings and openings on the leeward side. 'Perflation' is the effect of the wind blowing through a building from side to side, or end to end.

Stack effect The principal requirement here is a ventilator arrangement at the highest point of the building which may be permanently open, as with most 'open ridge' arrangements, or may be controlled, as with outlet ventilator trunks or chimney ventilators. The former system is normally used in the case of adult cattle, pigs, or sheep, whilst the latter arrangement is better suited for younger animals for which a finer control is required. Designs of both are shown in Figs. 7.1, 7.2 and 7.3. The ideal arrangement for 'stack effect' ventilation is a building with a pitched roof no more than about 15 m wide and with a steep slope on each side, thus helping the air upwards. Tables 7.1 and 7.2 give essential figures for installing ventilation systems.

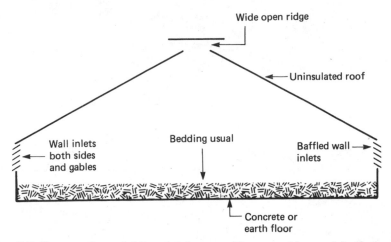

Fig. 7.1 Cross-section of 'climatic' house with open ridge and baffled wall ventilation

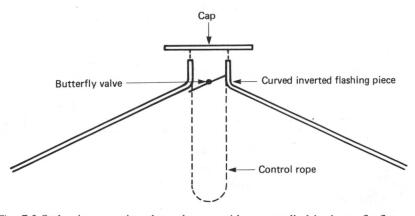

Fig. 7.2 Stale air extraction through open ridge controlled by butterfly flap

Table 7.1 Minimum area for the outlet of stale air in farm buildings

Type of building	Minimum outlet area (m²/animal)
Cows	0.09
Farrowing pigs	0.01
Fattening pigs	0.008
Calves	0.006
Laying birds	0.003
Broiler poultry	0.0015

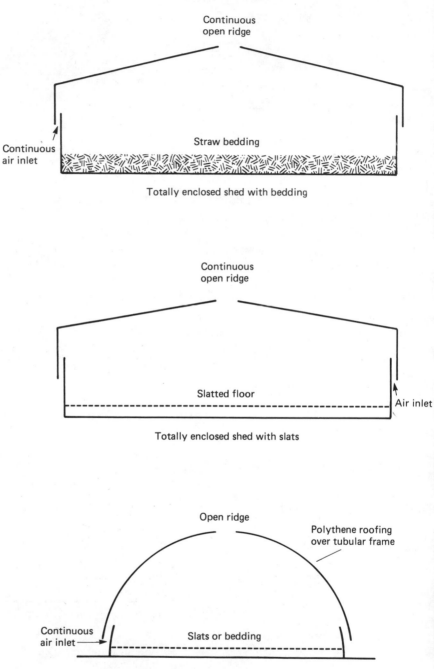

Fig. 7.3 Various types of naturally ventilated buildings

Table 7.2 Ventilation rates for varying conditions in temperate climates for farm livestock

Animal	(m³/hour/kg body weight)	
	Maximum summer rate	Minimum winter rate
Adult cattle	0.75–1.4	0.19
Young calf	0.94–1.9	0.38
Sow and litter	0.94–1.9	0.38
Fattening pig	0.94–1.9	0.38
Broiler chicken	2.8 –4.7	0.75
Laying poultry	5.6 –9.4	1.50

A more difficult problem is encountered with buildings wider than this, and especially if the slope is shallow, or a 'saw-tooth' or multiple ridge roof arrangement is used. In this case natural ventilation can be achieved most satisfactorily by using a 'breathing roof' (Fig. 7.4) either with gaps between the roof sheeting or with the sheets kept apart at the overlap by wooden spacers. This system is not controllable and so is only satisfactory for older or hardier bovine, porcine or ovine animals.

The advantage of the chimney ventilator, apart from its easy regulation with a slide, flap or butterfly valve (which may be controlled by a thermostat) is that it can be readily insulated by constructing it in timber and/or with an insulation lining, and it

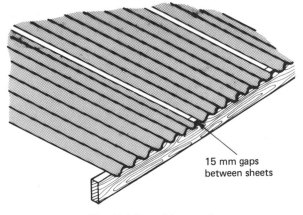

15 mm gaps
between sheets

Fig. 7.4 Breathing roof

will hence keep the air warm as it passes upwards so that it retains its 'light' properties. The true fixed open ridge with an uninsulated roof is the simplest form of extraction ventilation but it will not work very efficiently on a damp, warm, windless day whereas the chimney ventilator will still be quite good. The efficiency of both systems is greatly helped by insulating the roof. There are various ways of doing this, either letting the insulation follow the line of the roof or by a partly flat or totally flat ceiling, the two latter arrangements being especially favoured for very lofty buildings. The chimney trunks may finish near the ridge, flush with the ceiling, or may be brought down into the house near the floor in order to scavenge the foul air near animal level (Fig. 7.5). Whilst this has some advantages, it tends to get in the way of cleaning operations.

With regard to the inlet arrangements, there are a considerable number to choose from. For adults, where regulation is unnecessary but draughts must be avoided, the most suitable arrangement is spaced boarding (often called Yorkshire boarding) which is illustrated in Fig. 7.6. Boards are placed with carefully calculated gaps to allow air in and out but prevent draughts, rain and snow entry. Such an arrangement can be placed around the sides and ends of the house. Buildings that are exposed require less of this arrangement than those in protected areas. There are also very useful proprietary louvred metal sheets, e.g. the Ventair, which can be used as an even more efficient alternative. For younger stock it is better to have regulation on the inlets and these may be in the form of inward opening hoppers or sliding spaced boarding to give a variable opening of the gaps. Farmers really do not like using controllable inlets but they are far better where younger stock are concerned.

Aspiration The system we have so far described for ventilation will be complemented by the aspirating effect of the wind, especially with the designs of open ridge shown. They are the ideal arrangement and are also complemented by having an inlet area some three times the outlet area and uniformly distributed round the building.

Perflation In the cold weather a main ventilating force is the 'stack effect' but as weather warms up this becomes less and less important and eventually disappears altogether. The wind

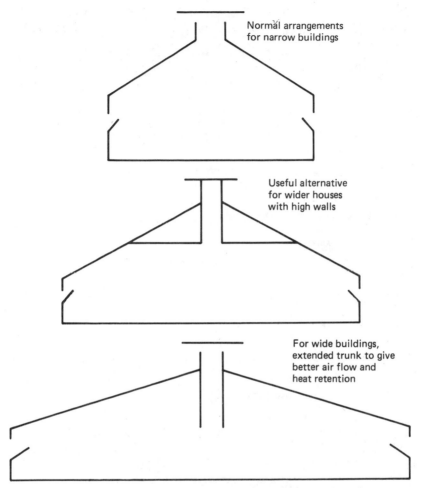

Normal arrangements
for narrow buildings

Useful alternative
for wider houses
with high walls

For wide buildings,
extended trunk to give
better air flow and
heat retention

Fig. 7.5 Alternative arrangements for outlet trunks and roofs

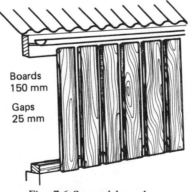

Boards
150 mm

Gaps
25 mm

Fig. 7.6 Spaced boards

effects of aspiration and perflation then take over and are critical. The existing systems so far described are perfectly able to function in this respect with the special attention to be paid to the utmost regulation to give a large measure of perflation. In many cases in really hot weather doors are opened to be replaced by wire grids if necessary and it is helpful if large areas of the sides, whether of spaced boarding or of ventilators, can be totally removed to cope with such conditions. The precise area that needs to be removable will depend on the location of the building and the type and density of the stock kept therein.

The use of thermal insulation

In its simplest form, the naturally ventilated or climatic building is an uninsulated structure used by animals which can withstand normal fluctuations in temperature but in which there is normally copious bedding. If, however, the animals are kept without litter, for example on slatted floors, even though they may be fairly hardy animals there is very likely to be a need for insulation to keep them warmer and prevent condensation. Really good insulation on the roof in particular will have the great additional advantage of helping the air flow by maintaining the warmth of the air as it passes towards the roof opening(s). However, the use of natural ventilation is no longer confined.to the 'climatic' house; it is now becoming widely used, if not preferred, for the controlled environment house. Good thermal insulation is the key to this type of building: stocking density will probably be high and the air flow must be kept going at all times. In fact, with the right shape of building and a very high standard of insulation, cold weather air flow is usually not difficult. A much greater problem is the hot weather, and this is usually where the building succeeds or fails. A high standard of thermal insulation clearly reduces heat transfer from without to within in the hot summer days. The problems of heat stress are also helped by having a light reflective roof, such as a bright metallic finish, and also a good overhang on the eaves to protect the walls from the heat of the midday sun (Fig. 7.7).

Ventilating the monopitch house

The virtues of the monopitch (or lean-to) house have been

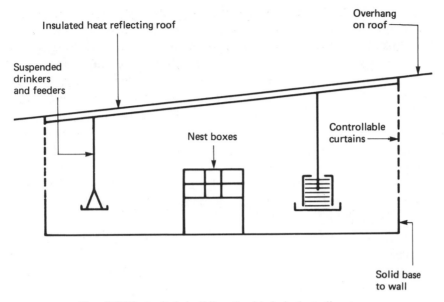

Fig. 7.7 Monopitch building for birds in hot climates

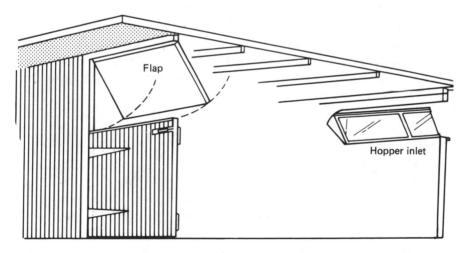

Fig. 7.8 Monopitch profile

widely appreciated (Fig. 7.8). The ventilation method is quite the simplest. A steep pitch on the sloping roof with a simple controllable flap at the front and at the back is the limit of the required air flow.

The cost of naturally ventilated housing

It must be stressed that it is not a main plank of the argument for naturally ventilated buildings that they are cheaper in capital cost. What is saved in the simplicity of construction may be lost in the necessity of providing the animals with a more generous amount of space. The extra space cannot be safely sacrificed for ecomony's sake. It is necessary in such housing to have a lower stocking rate to allow the animals some choice in their position in the building and thereby give some assurance against extremes. So the cost per animal may be much the same as in a controlled environment house. However, the running costs must be less as there is little or no electric power to use either on ventilation or lighting. There are also likely to be some tangible advantages in terms of productivity and health by giving the animals extra space.

The main advantage, which is much less tangible, is in a greater assurance that the animals will be all right whether there is the immediate presence of the stockman or not. The advantage of 'Peace of Mind' can hardly be estimated! Where laudable economies can be made is in the construction of the building, especially with the monopitch house. This is the simplest of all buildings to erect and is the easiest for the do-it-yourself erector. The surface area per animal is also far less than in the totally enclosed building.

The fan and the thermostat

Over the past forty years the livestock industry has increasingly taken the view that the best way to achieve the correct ventilation is by mechanical means using electric fans controlled by various thermostatic devices and ensuring that the air is moved at most times in this way. The problem with such arrangements is that the fan capacity that must be put in to cope with the greatest stocking density and the warmest weather is well above that required when the animals are small and the weather is cold. Thus, the ratio of maximum to minimum is very great. For example, in a fattening piggery it could be about 40:1, and in a broiler chicken house as much as 200:1. Because of the necessity for achieving a high degree of automatic control, reliance is usually placed on thermostats but these must always be considered only as aids and not as the total means of control. Consider Table 7.2, which shows the rates of air flow required by livestock of different types. These figures are based at the summer rates on the need to keep ambient temperatures within the house within a degree or two of the outside environment, and the minimum winter rate is sufficient to eliminate from the building all the moisture produced by the animals' excretions and expirations. This rate, in the absence of scientific evidence not yet available, is logical and in practice satisfactory and should remove the pathogenic micro-organisms produced in the respiratory system which are potentially very dangerous.

The point that must be made is that the animal is producing these organisms and respiring all the time and therefore any system which intermittently shuts off all ventilation is not advisable. The principal requirement must be to have a system which uses a thermostat only to assist the temperature control at the upper end of the scale *above* the minimum needed to get rid of all the pollutants in the environment. This minimum figure will be largely related to the size and weight of the livestock and will have to be adjusted accordingly. Devices which control the ventilation by time-cycles, which sometimes have all the ventilation and at other times none, are very dangerous.

The complexities of ventilation regulation are clearly not inconsiderable, adding to the cost of environmental control both in capital and running cost terms, and also making it quite difficult for the stockman to know whether the system is working or not. It is also necessary to have some failsafe device with a mechanical system so that if the power or the fans fail, there is an emergency arrangement, either through a diesel standby generator, or by some device which opens up the house for natural air flow, at least to suffice until the mechanical system can be restored (see Fig. 7.9). All these complexities and costs have led to a return to natural ventilation systems wherever possible and, interestingly, even housing systems which at one time it was considered could only be served by mechanical systems, such as broiler chicken houses and slatted floor piggeries, have now been found to be quite satisfactorily served by natural flow.

It must be emphasised that, if required, natural ventilation can be regulated by thermostatic devices, with the thermostats activating motors to open and close the ventilating flaps. These

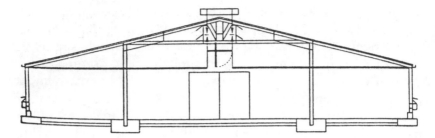

Fig. 7.9 The failsafe system consists of: Electromagnetic failsafe system to base of fan trunk and top of outlet box (pivot at base); Weather sealing to joint between outlet box and wall; Back-draught shutters of 1 000 gauge reinforced polythene sheet; Vermin-proof grid to airway from outlet box; Airways to be not less than 0.1 m^2/1500 m^3h except at fan; Maximum airway to fan back-draught shutters: 1½ × fan area; Fan mounting as manufacturer's specification of diaphragm ring and running mode for maximum volume output

devices have certain inherent risks, as with all thermostatic devices, but it is quite possible to have them regulated so a basic flow is always achieved regardless of temperature. Systems of thermostatic control of ventilator flaps are known as Automatically Controlled Natural Ventilation (ACNV).

Natural lighting

In recent years there has been a pronounced trend towards the use of dim lighting in windowless buildings with a total reliance on artificial lighting. This has had profound effects on the methods of husbandry and in consequence on the welfare of the stock and also on the economics of livestock rearing. As mentioned earlier, artificial lighting tends not to be as pleasant for working conditions and may make good hygiene and inspection of the animals less effective. The extra costs of equipment and electricity with the use of artificial lighting are obvious.

In practice there is little difficulty in providing natural lighting in most animal buildings both economically and efficiently. In 'controlled environment' animal houses, or indeed any house where there is good insulation, the area of translucent material is obviously a weak point for heat loss and gain, but this difficulty may be largely overcome (a) by using a double thickness of material with air space between (simple double glazing), and (b) wherever feasible, by utilising the windows or glazed area as part of the ventilation system. For example, there is no better window or fresh air inlet for most buildings than the inward opening, bottom-hinged hopper window, opening between gussets. Many other ventilation arrangements in fact allow the entry of a great deal of light, such as most open ridges, or the 'breathing roofs' (see Fig. 7.4), or Yorkshire or space-boarding (see Fig. 7.6).

8 Kennel Housing

Animal welfare attempts to provide a farm animal with an environment which satisfies most of the normal behavioural needs of the animal and protects it from factors of stress as we currently understand it. It is one of the features of the totally enclosed house that with modern husbandry requirements the building tends to be large and the number of animals kept together in groups is substantial. These cause many difficulties, which have been touched on earlier. In large groups there is a considerable opportunity for bullying, which has serious immediate effects on the welfare of the animals, but may also tend to lead to vices. Animals in large groups may also suffer from environmental problems. It may be difficult for all the animals to position themselves in the best conditions – the environment is rarely totally uniform. In any event, animals do not require the same conditions when they are resting as when they are moving around. A cooler, or more variable environment is perfectly satisfactory for the latter. It is also quite illogical to provide a controlled environment for the area in which the animals move around and for that which contains the faeces and urine. Above all, as we have seen, there will be great advantages from the health aspect in placing animals in small groups by one method or another, and this is where the kennel arrangement tends to have all the advantages. It does not, of course, provide complete isolation of one group from another, but it goes a very long way towards it in practical terms, which are often enough. The faeces and urine may drain out of a pen to a gully in front but outside the pen itself, so there is no inter-pen contact in this respect. Then, with solid partitions between each pen, the only air that passes between the pens will have to go from a pen, outside into the open and round the corner back into the next pen. If one is dealing with a highly contagious disease then this barrier would obviously form no real check.

But in practice the type of problems usually encountered are due very much more to the pressure of a high number of challenging organisms together with an animal that is severely weakened by a poor environment. Thus the isolation is well worth the effort.

For reasons which are far from understood but which are real enough from all the evidence, animals thrive much better in smaller groups; perhaps they feel more secure and less threatened. Thus it seems that the kennel arrangement has much to commend it for many types of animal.

Let us now look at the essentials of design. It is highly desirable that, so far as possible, all kennel houses face one way – in a southerly direction. With this arrangement, the animals can move towards the front in the sunny warm weather and have the benefit of the best conditions, or move to the back parts when the weather is cooler. Because the housing tends to be of relatively low cost, the animals can have more generous space allowances to give them a freedom of choice, whilst, because they are in small groups, it is not too risky for their health to allow them to bunch together in fairly tight groups to keep warm.

Many farmers make the mistake of placing rows of kennels or monopitch houses face to face. This is to be avoided, since not only will one side receive little or no sun and also be facing into the coldest winds, but the passageway between the two facing rows becomes something of a wind tunnel and can make the environment unsatisfactory at certain times for both stock and stockmen.

A very important feature of the kennel house is the way in which it ensures that each pen of animals may be quite undisturbed by what goes on in the next pen. For example, if there are a number of pens in a row, pigs can be put in or taken out of a pen without any interference from or to the others, which makes management very much easier.

Constructional costs can be kept down in a number of ways. The procedure in most monopitch or kennel buildings is to have the whole area totally covered but in some cases it is considered perfectly satisfactory, if not better, to have only part of the building covered – what may be termed the lying area. Thus, in monopitch cattle housing there may be an uncovered yarded area in front of the lying area, where the cattle will feed and exercise. This can be of much benefit to health and to the acclimatisation of the animals. With pigs it is even better because it gives them the opportunity to behave in a natural way, this being to stay mainly in the cover of a true kennel but to defecate, urinate and feed outside the area. The absence of any pollution, other than respiratory, in the kennel area helps to keep the animals healthy, whilst the excreta is much more easily cleaned when it is in an outside yard, often by simply washing down with a pressure hose. It is not without significance that pigs kept in these forms of housing rarely show any tendency to vices and there is a minimum of fighting. This illustrates that it is likely that the pigs are in close harmony with their environment.

Kennel housing for some stock should be thermally insulated, at least so far as the lying area is concerned. This applies generally to all ages of pigs, the buildings usually being of quite low construction so that without insulation there is a risk of condensation, and temperature fluctuation may be excessive. However, with the much loftier monopitch housing used for cattle, in which eaves height may well be as much as 4 metres, the effect of the insulation is rather lost and the extra protection required for the younger stock is more sensibly achieved by having a restricted area at the back temporarily roofed with timber and straw which is easily dismantled for cleaning.

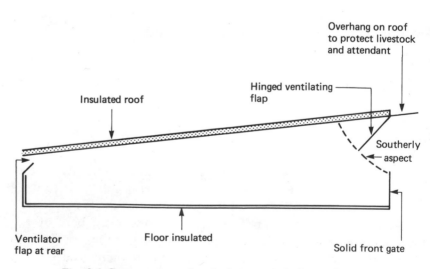

Fig. 8.1 Cross-section of typical monopitch (kennel) house

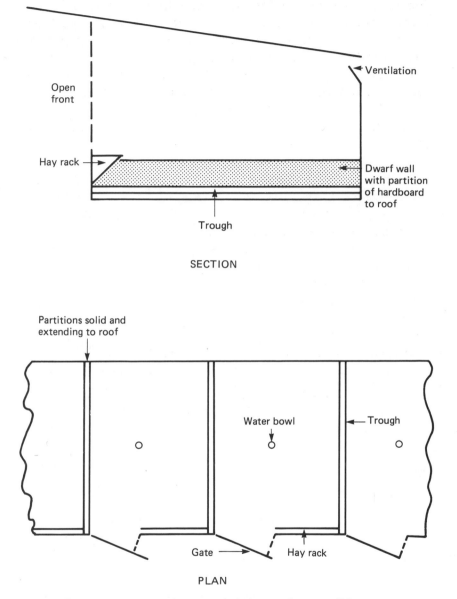

Fig. 8.2 An economic monopitch for ruminants calf house

Typical profiles are shown in Figs. 8.1, 8.2 and 8.3. For pigs, a low back and steep pitch on the roofs assist with the air flow. The only ventilation is usually achieved by having a hopper flap at the rear, which must be very tight fitting to avoid draughts

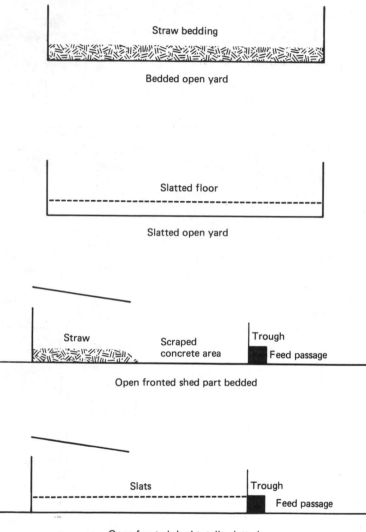

Fig. 8.3 Simple roofless and monopitch livestock housing suitable for ruminants

when closed during cool weather, and a large flap in front, to be hinged back under the ceiling progressively as more ventilation is required. With calves a somewhat similar design may be used, but with older cattle it is usually a shallow pitch, as the back may already be quite high enough and in any case there is no need to try and retain heat in such a building. With this type of building, as with all 'kennels', the front is the only area normally open, but with the cattle building large flaps are cumbersome and impractical and Netlon is a much better protector.

9 Welfare and Flooring

The flooring of the intensive animal house constitutes one of the major problems in the animal welfare field. Many welfarists insist that the best or indeed the only acceptable type of flooring is a bed of straw or similar type of material, corresponding more or less with the natural surface most animals would lie on. There can certainly be little question that such a bed would be ideal, but it is a simplification of the art of rearing animals to believe this is the only surface that can be used.

Let us consider some of the essentials of management if animals are kept on straw or bedding. The straw must be sufficiently copious in quantity to provide a dry underfoot surface and to absorb immediately free urine or wet faecal material. Whilst a floor that is kept in a good state may be ideal, a badly maintained bedded floor can be as bad as any. If there is insufficient bedding it becomes wet and the animal becomes wet and dirty with urine and faeces. Such an environment is usually not only physiologically stressful by virtue of the extra sensation of cold, but it also acts as an ideal medium for the perpetuation of harmful micro-organisms. Good examples of the diseases that are promoted by such conditions are the so-called environmental mastitis of dairy cows – especially associated with dirty bedding in cubicles; 'farrowing fever' in sows associated especially with dirty sows in pregnancy and in the farrowing house; and finally in poultry, wet litter producing the ideal conditions for the multiplication and challenge to the birds of *E. coli* septicaemia. Also, with litter wet with excreta there are likely to be considerable effusions of ammonia and this may have a harmful effect on the animals' resistance to respiratory infections.

There are essentially two ways of managing bedding when used in animal accommodation. It may be put into the pen (frequently) *and be cleaned out completely*, so maintaining the bed in a healthy state by regularity. This is an expensive procedure, not only on the bedding but much more so on labour, and so tends not to be favoured in the intensive unit. Where it is used is in the housing of horses where economics are at a different level altogether! The alternative procedure, more favoured, is to attempt the separation of the animal from its own excreta by a regular 'topping up' operation with bedding added almost daily so that the animal has a dry and clean bed to lie on. This is fine and much favoured with housing sytems for every type of animal but is a danger if the bedding runs short and the animal lies in what is in fact a manure heap.

A principal need if this system is to be satisfactory is for the supply of bedding to be copious – some might say 'vast' – otherwise it can be a disaster; and in addition, special arrangements must be made for the 'build-up' of the litter until the animals are cleared out and the whole lot is removed by some mechanically-aided method.

Those who so passionately advocate bedded systems must appreciate the considerable expense involved in gathering or purchasing the straw or other form of litter, in storage and handling, and eventually in disposal. But there are two great advantages. Firstly, the environmental conditions may be enormously helped. As soon as an animal has access to bedding it is in a position to take an active part in the control of its own environment. There is dryness, comfort, and warmth in good bedding so that the control of the rest of the environment may be very much less exacting and precise and the insulation and ventilation of the house can be effected on simpler lines. Furthermore, it is not feasible or really necessary to house the animals so densely when they are kept on bedding and this will relieve the system of some of the tensions that cause trouble. Obviously, by spreading the animals over a larger area there is less likelihood of disease, especially those conditions that have been emphasised earlier which tend to be rife in intensive units and which are caused by the challenge of potential pathogens. The extra space will also be of help in avoiding vices, and with bedding provided, and assuming it is of good quality, the boredom that is believed to be one of the main causes of vices has diminished too, since animals will play with, eat, scratch, or dust-bathe in suitable material. Bedding will also help as part of the diet. It is hardly to be claimed that this is a central reason for providing bedding, but it is certainly the case in our present state of knowledge that the extra fibre that may be needed by animals and which is not found in their ration is taken by them with alacrity from the bedding.

The second great advantage of using bedding is that it is one way in which it is possible to dispose of muck in solid rather than slurry form. Though the removal of the muck may be, even by mechanical means, quite a laborious process, nevertheless, once removed, it is easy to store for as long as desired and is then used with great advantage on the land which it almost invariably improves. This is very different from the disposal of slurry which, whilst it is relatively easy to handle, given a fairly substantial outlay on capital equipment, is expensive to store and does not provide the same quality of material for the land; it also has a greater number of disease hazards unless it is held for a substantial length of time. It is also of note that slurry disposal can be a great nuisance to the human population, since the smell is often exceedingly foul and can spread downwind several miles from the area of application. Several cases have gone through the Courts where orders have been given to close down such units.

Alternatives to bedding

It can be seen that it is considered best if the housed animal is bedded on some straw or other suitable material, but for all the reasons stated it is not by any means everyone's choice for keeping the stock. One search with modern systems is for arrangements which ensure a comfortable, healthy and more or less trouble-free floor without the time-hungry, diligent management and expertise which is required in bedded pens. Furthermore, it must be appreciated that in many areas of the world it is necessary to keep animals but bedding is virtually unobtainable. Maintaining stock on bare concrete or timber floors has long been practised but is not a particularly successful technique, for the floor easily becomes wet, and this is a very inhospitable if not cruel surface to the animals, easily causing injury and abrasions, and also inclined to chill. If the slope on the floor is made steep it will be drier, but the animal will be inclined to slip. On the other hand if the floor is made quite flat, then the moisture will be retained and there will certainly be harmful results. There is therefore usually no bare floor that is very satisfactory as a bed, unless it is with the pig which has the desire to keep its bed clean if given the opportunity and may lie comfortably enough if the floor is skilfully designed and constructed. But it is in the perforated, slatted or slotted floor that the true answer lies to the problem of a bare floor which is yet hygienic and healthy.

There is a belief that these are rather recent inventions but this is far from true. Both in this country and elsewhere they have been used for hundreds of years and often with apparently good success. Traditionally, the perforated floor was made with wooden slats, these being from 1–6 inches wide, and with a gap from a fraction of an inch up to about 1 inch.

Developments since then have seen floors produced in concrete, cast iron, steel, wire, plastic, timber, aluminium and other metals, with a huge variety of arrangements and perforations (Fig. 9.1 illustrates a well-designed concrete slat). The aim is always the same, however: to produce a durable and comfortable floor which disposes of the excreta automatically from the animal to a pit or channel underneath. In mammals the excreta, a mixture of faeces and urine, is usually a semi-liquid or slurry and can be disposed of by pump, if necessary adding some water. In poultry the product of the cloaca is solid and is usually disposed of in solid form.

There are certain enormous advantages of the perforated floor. Correctly designed, it appears to be comfortable to the

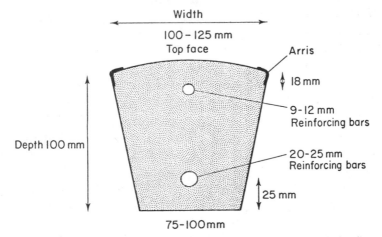

Fig. 9.1 An ideal concrete slat for pigs: cambered top, rounded edges and tapered profile

animal and by virtue of the immediate or rapid disposal of the excreta, keeps the animal clear of contact with its own excreta. The atmosphere may also be freer from pollution. These two features alone must have contributed to the good health of countless animals and have been one of the major reasons for improving health in young animals. For, whilst it is equally possible to keep good health in young animals by providing plenty of clean bedding at a regular and constant rate, it is much more difficult to do so, and the perforated floor achieves the end very much more reliably.

But against these advantages we have to weigh in with the drawbacks. The ideal of a comfortable floor may be completely absent in this arrangement and animals may suffer discomfort or injury from poorly designed or manufactured materials. Also, in order to be reasonably assured that the floor is self-cleaning, the animals must be packed in quite tightly and there is always a rather thin margin between what constitutes a reasonable density and over-stocking. There is a further danger of gases rising from the slurry and this causing distress, disease or death to the animals or the stockman. Also, bedding can only rarely be used on the slatted or perforated floors – by and large it is either impossible or it destroys the whole advantage of such a floor by clogging the slats or the disposal system. This means that there is the risk of boredom, or lack of useful activity, and much greater likelihood of vice. With animals exposed entirely to the environment there is clearly a much greater need for them to be kept in carefully regulated conditions and usually this means a sophisticated, controlled environment house with mechanical ventilation.

Hence it is clear that it is difficult to take too dogmatic a view about the whole question of flooring and slats. Some examples will serve to clarify the position. Generally speaking, whenever milking cattle have been kept on totally slatted floors in yarded accommodation, the result has been very unsatisfactory, especially in larger units. Injuries to the teats are sometimes extremely serious when a cow treads on the teat of another cow lying on the slats and it is often difficult to keep the cows clean enough to give hygienic milk production. Even with slats used only in the passages behind cubicles the results have been similar. Yet cows kept in small groups in warm and cosy accommodation, quietly managed, give superb results, especially if the slats are well designed such as those shown in Fig. 9.1. Likewise with beef animals, when the slats are properly designed and the animals kept in small groups, evenly matched for size, they appear to rear very comfortably and it would seem difficult to justify a wholesale condemnation *per se* of all types of cattle kept on slats, provided the design is good, the building suitable, the groups equable and the animals provided with adequate space.

Slatted floors have been responsible for the great success of earlier weaning of young piglets. When weaning at 3–4 weeks was first practised on solid floored pens, with or without bedding, it was usually a dismal failure due to the challenge of disease and especially enteric infections. However, with the onset and use of perforated flooring, the whole system became remarkably successful. Some pens are totally perforated, others have a solid area sometimes with bedding, but with a perforated exercising and dunging area. The choice of materials is enormous, ranging from hard plastic to metal and concrete, with a great variety in both size and shape of slats. Some forms, such as plastic or punched metal, appear to be 'kinder' to the piglets' feet but there is little evidence of any strong preference by the piglets. It is noteworthy that the second group of diseases that are of great economic importance so far as the young pig is concerned, is the respiratory group, especially rhinitis. In the flat-deck (described in Chapter 12), provided the ventilation is adequate, there is less aggravation from dust and so this disease which is apparently triggered by irritation by dust does tend to be much less prevalent.

In the early days of the flat-deck, certain types of flooring, especially metal ones, could cause overt damage to the piglets but since the unacceptable forms were identified, later sorts have provided a comfortable, healthy and successful floor for rearing piglets. Nevertheless doubts will remain as to whether it is humane to deny the piglets bedding, bearing in mind especially that the piglets will never have had access to it.

A much more difficult problem relates to the calf, and in particular the veal calf, which is reared in a slatted floor crate, also in dim conditions, and without any room to turn round or adequately groom itself.

The objects of rearing veal calves in this way are several. Firstly, the calves are traditionally fed an all-liquid diet of milk substitute so that their excreta is largely liquid. If they are housed on slats the excreta is easily disposed of by the usual methods of slurry disposal. By keeping the calves in a pen or stall that is too narrow to allow them to turn round they cannot foul their feeding utensils. One of the greatest hazards of calf rearing is the bacterial infection, especially Salmonella, which can run riot in a calf unit and which spreads by contact, largely via the faeces. By rearing the calves in crates this is virtually prevented as there is a minimal chance of spread from faecal contamination. The same can be said of other diseases, including respiratory infections.

The use of crates in small groups of 10–15 calves to a room is a very successful method of rearing veal calves, with many rearers recording losses of as little as 2%, compared with normal losses of 5–10%. It must be stressed that a principal reason why calves have been reared in this way is to ensure that they get no roughage and are fed a diet with low, or at least controlled, amounts of iron so as to produce the so-called 'white veal' required by the specialised trade. However, in more recent times, it has been shown that perfectly acceptable veal can be produced without such questionable dietary manipulations. Nor is it in any way necessary to keep calves in artificial conditions of high temperature and high humidity in order to produce top quality veal and it is quite feasible to rear them in almost traditional straw yarded pens where they will be subjected to the normal range of temperatures and they will also be able to eat roughage. Suitable designs are shown in Fig. 13.7 and the complete system is described in Chapter 13. Thus the 'alternative system', which in this case is, to some extent a reversion to the simpler and more traditional arrangement, has exposed as completely unfounded several widely held maxims for the production of veal which had never been scientifically proven.

10 Care of Sick Animals, Emergencies, Companionship and Mutilations

There was once a tradition of giving sick animals special 'environmental' care but this has largely passed in modern intensivism where so many animals are under the care of one attendant that special management may be difficult or impossible to institute. Apart from this there is a much greater reliance on the use of drugs and medical aids rather than on good management. This will obviously be understood to be a great pity since attention to management usually costs little and always does some good, whereas the use of drugs may be both costly and ineffective. *At its best, however, a good environment aids the ability of the drugs to achieve their aims.*

When animals are sick they tend to huddle together in small groups to keep warm. This can be unsatisfactory because it tends to exacerbate the disease problem by creating a heavily polluted environment around the animals. Sick animals often 'run a temperature' and will therefore feel the cold. Thus for both the foregoing reasons it is frequently beneficial if some extra warmth is applied to the stock. They will be more inclined to disperse in their accommodation and encourage a healthier environment. Whilst artificial means of warming the air, such as electric infra-red lamps, gas radiant heaters or fan heaters, are all quick and handy ways of providing the heat, much can equally well be done by the installation of cosy insulated 'kennels' within a building, which conserve the animal's warmth and reduce draught. One way in which the warmth must not be generated is purely by restriction of the ventilation – this can obviously be very harmful by increasing the challenge of pathogens on the animals.

Another way of aiding sick animals is to ensure they have comfortable flooring. Sick animals often scour and fail to keep themselves clean so they become dirty and thereby add to their own infection. Much help may be achieved by moving the sick animals to a clean and deeply bedded pen – this assists in environment and health equally.

Isolation accommodation

A sick animal tends to get bullied or even killed by the healthy stock, so for its own good it may need to be removed. It can then be given any special treatment required, saving the unnecessary medication of others when treatment is given *en masse*. At the same time by removing the sick animals a certain extra challenge on the healthy stock is automatically removed. Isolation is needed for parturition – and is usually provided – but it can also be of considerable assistance to the undersized. Emphasis is constantly placed on the value of ensuring uniform groups in pens of animals but, even if this is particularly well achieved, there comes a time when certain animals may benefit by being removed from the group to separate accommodation. This not only helps the small animals, it helps the larger ones by giving them more space and it also enables pens to be cleared more precisely in order to give time for cleaning and disinfection and a short period of rest.

With isolation accommodation there is also the possibility of giving the animal the more personal attention that it may need. Partly this may mean the possibility of easier handling for injections, treatment of wounds or injuries, but it also means that the sick animal will have easier access to feed and water, and applies very much to the environmental requirements. If the sick animals are removed they can more readily be given the specific environment they may need. For all these reasons there is no difficulty in justifying the case for isolation accommodation as an essential for all livestock units – and in practice, one that is frequently neglected.

Emergency coverage

By and large, the more traditional systems of husbandry do not have the hazards found in the modern intensive systems. In the intensive house, power failure or mechanical breakdown can lead to the total stoppage of all ventilation. It may also stop feed and water supplies or mechanised cleaning arrangements. If there is a slurry disposal into a tank under slats, ventilation failure can lead to gases creeping into the building. If lighting fails in a windowless building the animals may panic. The other great risk in the intensive building is that of fire, since it is extremely difficult to move stock when they are frightened by the presence of fire and there are frequent cases of whole buildings full of livestock perishing when a fire occurs.

It is an alarming fact that there have been a number of disasters to my knowledge when a blow-lamp has been used to thaw out frozen water pipes, and the building has been destroyed, usually through hay or straw catching light. It is rarely appreciated how highly combustible hay and straw becomes after it has been in a building for some time. It is very common to see, for example, wires draped across a house or pen to serve an infra-red lamp for pigs. The lamp or wires can sometimes be interfered with by the sow, at other times the lamp may be knocked or may fall onto a straw bed – all being major fire risks. Open wiring of this sort is also very vulnerable to the attention of rats and mice and as it is often run across a temporary straw-covered creep or nest top, the risks are enormous.

Another emergency which it is most important to consider is that of providing food and water during very bad winter weather, especially deep snow. It is of course most likely that animals under outdoor, especially free-range conditions, will suffer most severely from bad weather, but there have also been considerable problems with intensive units cut off by snow from feed supplies.

Thus it is necessary to do everything possible when planning the enterprise to safeguard the animals and the following are some of the measures that may be taken:

1. Alarm systems which warn the person in charge of a failure of the electrical supply to a building and to equipment are available quite cheaply; both these and automatic fire alarm systems can ensure speedy action is taken.
2. Wherever the ventilation system is totally dependent on a power supply then normal planning must provide an alternative for use in the event of mains supply failure. In large units this is usually done by installing a stand-by generator which automatically cuts in when electrical current fails. If this is uneconomic an alternative is to have an arrangement

whereby 'natural' ventilation can be used to cope with the circumstance for a limited period. This is usually done by the attendant opening up a number of special flaps or doors when the mains failure alarm is set off, but in some cases an automatic arrangement is used. It is done in this way: a number of ventilators are placed in the house which are closed off when the fans are working but the flaps that close them are held in place by electro-magnets (see Fig. 7.9). The moment the power fails the flaps open and stay open until they are closed again after the power is restored. Nevertheless, it may be pointed out that because of the emergencies that may occur due to power or fan failure and because a dual system is expensive, there is much to be said for using wherever possible a ridge extraction arrangement which, even in the absence of fans, will give a good measure of ventilation. Many power supply failures are associated with blizzards, snow storms and ice, and at such times there may be little need for the fans at all if the arrangement is designed as a fan-assisted naturally ventilated arrangement.

3. Electric light failure may be coped with either by generator, battery set, or the use of special window lights. It is important, too, to train animals to darkness, so they do not panic, by giving them from their youngest days certain periods of darkness. There is, however, much wisdom in having windows in all animal housing, even though it may be of modest amount (see Chapter 7).

4. Fire is a more difficult hazard to cope with. Animals such as birds in battery cages will take a very long time to take out and represent the greatest hazard. Fire creates such stress and fear in animals that they tend to stay immobile, or may even run back into the building after being released. Thus much depends on planning – dividing a building with fireproof materials, using fireproof materials generally, protecting electrical wiring from damage (short-circuiting is a common cause of fire) and taking the greatest care whenever naked flames are used, either in heaters or for any other purposes.

5. To avoid the risk of feed supplies being cut off by bad weather, some consideration should be given to this possibly when the unit is planned, avoiding the siting of large intensive units in inaccessible areas with poor access by food

lorries and other essential transport. A further precaution is to be certain that there are substantial reserves of food on the site when unfavourable weather conditions are expected.

Companionship in animals

It has often been stated as a fundamental truth that the greatest enemy of one animal is another. Perhaps this is true from the disease point of view, but it is not so from all the evidence when it comes to behaviour and comfort of animals. A good example of this misconception is with poultry. It is not many years ago that fowls were kept one bird to a cage, and the fact that this system had only a moderate following was only due to the very high capital cost. Almost by accident it was established that when two birds were put together in a cage, either the same size as a single birdcage or a little larger, each bird was more productive than when kept alone. Thus, in spite of some extra stress created by restricting the space allowance to the birds, this was apparently more than compensated for by the benefits of putting birds in close proximity.

There is also an interesting factor with regard to sows. Those kept in individual stalls over the period when they were required to be mated would often show poor reproductive activity both physiologically and behaviourally. It was subsequently discovered that this problem was created by the isolation and there was unlikely to be a difficulty if sows were in groups, and the response would be especially good if they were in sight, sound and smell of the boar. It has long been recognised in traditional livestock rearing that the isolated animal tends to be 'bad-tempered', or even savage, behaviour epitomised in the bull which was often located in a dark and unpleasant corner of the barn where it might see little of the farm's activity. The correct way to prevent this is to make sure that the bull is kept in the midst of activity, both human and animal, for it would then be unlikely to show the aberrant behaviour which is likely to be based on fear of the unknown and not on any inherent evil temper. There are good physiological reasons for putting animals together; by their disposition they may be able to counteract the adverse effects of cold, when they will tend to come together to keep warm, and in conditions of greater heat they will move apart to keep cool.

'Mutilation' of farm animals

It is generally accepted and is a main point in the UK Codes of Recommendations for the Welfare of Farm Livestock that unnecessary mutilation of farm animals should be avoided wherever possible. There are several important reasons for this which examples will make clear. The docking of pigs' tails when the piglet is young is a very common occurrence in order to avoid tail-biting during the fattening stage. Tail-biting is a most serious condition which can lead to great distress in the pigs and potentially damaging effects, both directly and indirectly, on the animals. If a method can be found of avoiding it, it is to be applauded. However, the disadvantage of tail docking is that there may be some pain in the carrying out of the action (though probably very slight and transitory) but, perhaps more import- antly, it does not tackle or remove the root cause of the problem. The result may then be that the 'discomforted' pig may resort to other aberrant behaviour, for example, biting the ears or other parts that cannot be removed, which may lead to complete cannibalism.

The complexities of this condition are, however, increased when it must further be admitted that the causes are not well understood and certainly appear to be due to many different aspects of husbandry which cause discomfort to the pig. Some of these may be listed: overcrowding, housing pigs of vastly different size together, poor ventilation, draughts, over-heating of the pigs, an absence of bedding, insufficient food, nutritional imbalances, low fibre in the food, diarrhoea, parasitism, skin infection, abrasions or any trauma on the pig leading to bleeding, excessive light or dark, and finally, certain inherent characteristics. This is not an exhaustive list but what it does show is that tail-biting may be said to be most probably due to some defect in husbandry.

Tail-biting is an indication that something is wrong, and whilst it is laudable to dock tails for a period to prevent injury, it is vital that this is considered only to be a transitory procedure whilst the factor in husbandry that caused it is examined.

Another example is the so-called de-beaking of chicken. Intensively housed poultry are strongly inclined to feather- pecking and sometimes also vent-pecking and more destructive forms of cannibalism. A method of preventing it is to trim the beak back so the danger is greatly reduced. The job is usually done soon after the chicks are hatched and may cause little pain, but a sensitive area of the beak has gone and the picking and selection of food may be impaired. It has also done nothing to remove the root cause. So, again, beak trimming may be looked upon as a transitory procedure pending an adjustment of the system to remove the danger. Factors behind the causes are somewhat similar to those leading to tail-biting in pigs, for example, an inherent tendency in certain strains, bullying, overcrowding, unevenness in the group, absence of or poor litter, excessive lighting, feed deficiencies or imbalances in quality or quantity, parasitism, poor growth, and deficiencies in ventilation or environmental control. The important fact to be aware of in both these examples is that there is always likely to be some defect in management behind the habit and it can be looked upon as a challenge to remove it.

11 Methods of Studying Farm Animal Welfare

Investigations into the welfare of farm animals come essentially under four headings. Firstly, there are the so-called 'preference' tests in which the animals make a choice between any number of environments and it is accepted that the choice is made because of the welfare considerations. Secondly, we can measure physiological responses such as the effects of stress reactions involving the activity of the pituitary adrenal axis (Dantzer *et al.*, 1983) or fear response (Duncan, 1983). Thirdly, there is consideration of the productivity of the livestock and, finally, their health, including not only recognition of diseases caused by pathogenic micro-organisms but also any defect arising from injury or abnormality due to faults in nutrition, genetics, management or housing.

Development of a Welfare Index

It must be made clear that there is limited value in any welfare investigation which considers only single dimensions of welfare. In order to overcome this disadvantage Baxter (1983) has suggested the development of a *Welfare Index* to which all welfare dimensions are referred. As he states, in theory at least, the welfare of an animal at a given point could be represented by a single value on this index. Also, entire environments could be compared in their total effects on welfare with reference to this Welfare Index. A great advantage of this method of comparing different welfare determinants is that it is predominantly animal-orientated, with a minimum of human interference and interpretation.

Very comprehensive investigations have elucidated the optimal environments for the different forms of animal production, in order to allow for the basic physiological needs of animals and also minimise the attendant's work. However, it has become more and more apparent during the last decades that providing a well-controlled environment is not sufficient and that modern housing conditions can be detrimental because they restrict basic behaviour needs: hens kept in battery cages can no longer dust-bathe, pigs kept on a slatted floor are unable to root, etc. Such deprivation of species' specific activities imposed by housing conditions, combined with possible physical injuries caused by poor quality and/or design of floor, pen walls, troughs or other pieces of farm equipment, have been claimed to cause intense suffering in farm animals. The problem with which we are now confronted is to assess objectively the intensity of suffering in farm animals and to determine the exact conditions which are responsible. With this knowledge alternative systems can be devised.

Poor productivity and ill health represent objective criteria which are relatively easy to assess, but their connection with environmental factors and specific faults in management or housing designs are not easy to establish, due to the fact that causal factors are not acting alone, but in combination. In spite of the evidence for the multifactorial aspects of management in producing diseases, many pathologists still tend to pay more attention to microbial agents than to predisposing factors arising from the housing conditions (Dantzer, et al. 1983).

There are many cases, however, in which physical health does not appear to be substantially altered. For example, veal calves can be fattened tied up on slatted floors or free on straw. There is no significant difference in the incidence of disease, nor in the performances between the two systems which could justify the choice of one system over the other. Another example is to consider caged chicken. Nearly all the evidence shows that layers in cages suffer *less* disease, *less* mortality and give higher productivity than any of the other systems. Reliance must therefore be placed on other factors in assessing welfare. The basic idea is that the higher the pressure exerted by the environment on the behaviour and physiology of the animals, the more profound the subsequent adaptive changes which will take place. So it can be predicted that by assessing adaptive changes occurring in animals given different management and housing conditions, it should be possible to tell how much pressure they have been submitted to. With this evidence it might be possible to make predictions of the adaptive abilities of a given breed of animal to a specific environment.

Physiological criteria and the biology of adaptation

Dantzer *et al.* (1983) have summarised this aspect of welfare investigation. As they say, adaptation is a dynamic process initiated by external or internal changes threatening the survival of the individual and his reproductive success. This process involves both behavioural and neuroendocrine adjustments and aims at decreasing the adverse consequences of challenge.

In reaction to impinging environmental stimulation the subject engages in specific behaviour and its hormonal state changes. Both types of response are not the result of a simple reflex action but involve central nervous processing of the sensory information according to the early experience and the individual's expectations. Hormones and behaviour are inter-related on at least two levels. Firstly, the individual's hormonal status when it enters the situation modulates the neural activity involved in the perception of the existing stimuli via the general metabolic state, the sensory receptors, and the brain itself. Secondly, both the experiences of the subject and the behaviour in which it engages produce changes in its hormonal state through a direct effect of behaviour on the existing stimulus, but also through the effects of these experiences and action on neural activity.

The model of hormone-behaviour interactions (Fig. 11.1) is important because it points out that study of the physiological correlation of adaptation is meaningless if the behavioural reactions are not assessed at the same time. This model also incorporates the notion that in many cases the success of adaptation depends on the opportunity for the animal to express the appropriate behavioural response. If animals are exposed to a cold draught they alter their position and seek shelter. However, if they cannot move away, they have to increase their heat production and decrease their heat losses in order to adjust to the draught. In other words, the basic adaptive response is behavioural, and the neuroendocrine changes which are going to take place are crucially dependent on the behavioural strategy adopted by the subject.

There are two fundamental neuroendocrine mechanisms which take part in adaptive processes – the pituitary-adrenal system, which gives rise to the general adaptation syndrome described by Selye (1936), and the sympathetic adrenal medul-

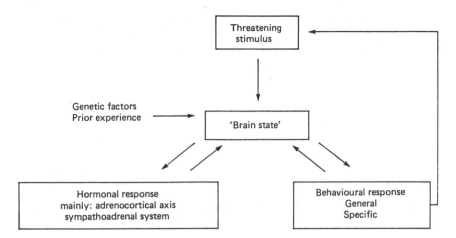

Fig. 11.1 Model of the relationship between environmental threatening stimuli and bodily responses. The responses which are initiated by the central nervous system depend on the 'brain state' at the time of stimulus perception. The behavioural response is given a specific quality aiming at the control of the threatening stimulus and a general quality which corresponds to two main modes of responding, either active (e.g. fight or flight) or passive (e.g. withdrawal, immobility or freezing). Peripherally released hormones depend on the behavioural attitude and they feed back to the brain to modulate the acquisition and retention of the behavioural response. (Dantzer, Mormède & Henry, 1983)

lary system described by Cannon (1935).

The pituitary-adrenal system is maximally activated under conditions of uncertainty, when coping attempts are thwarted and potentially disastrous threats are percieved which can neither be escaped nor controlled. The subject then tends to act in a passive way, with a predominance of submission and withdrawal. In contrast, security and sense of control are associated with low pituitary-adrenal activity (Henry and Stephens, 1977).

The sympathetic adrenal medullary system is activated when the power to control access to goal objects, such as food, water, shelter, mate and dependants, is challenged and leads to repeated attempts to maintain control. This response is associated with continued arousal and increase in heart rate, blood pressure and peripheral resistance. In contrast, the reverse trend, i.e. deactivation of the sympathetic adrenal medullary system, represents not just absence of effect but relaxations accompanying, for example, grooming and attachment behaviour.

The neurohormonal state of the individual at a given time can be represented as a point in a two-dimensional space, the coordinates of which correspond to two state variables defining respectively the pituitary-adrenal activity (horizontal axis) and the sympathetic adrenal medullary system (vertical axis), the centre defining the normal values of both variables in the population under study (Fig. 11.2).

The neurohormonal state of the animal changes continually due to the demands of the fluctuating external environment as well as to the intrinsic rhythmicity of the neuroendocrine systems. It is therefore more appropriate to describe a range of variation than a precise location in this two-dimensional space. Two types of changes can occur. Transitory changes are

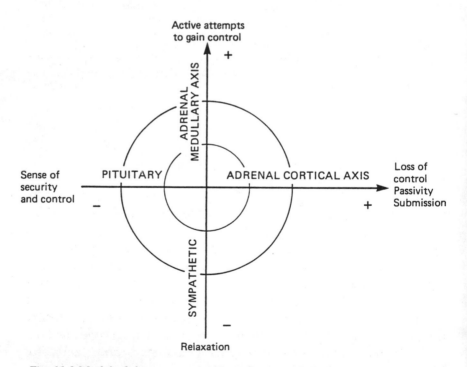

Fig. 11.2 Model of the neuroendocrine substrates of the emotional reactions to environmental stimulation. A sympathetic adrenal-medullary effort/relaxation axis is contrasted with a pituitary-adrenal-cortical loss of control/security axis in a two-dimensional space. The normal neuroendocrine activity of the population under study corresponds to the intersection of the two axes. (Dantzer, Mormède & Henry, 1983)

characterised by a displacement along one or two dimensions followed by a return to the normal fluctuation zone. In contrast, permanent changes implicate a new equilibrium among neuro-endocrine activities by changing hormonal set points.

Preference tests

The current status of preference testing in the assessment of animal welfare has been critically summarised by Dr. Marian Dawkins of Oxford University, who has herself carried out extensive and fundamental preference studies in poultry. As she states, a major problem in an assessment of farm management systems that takes account of the welfare of the animals is how to consult the animals themselves. However, a method of assessing animal welfare which is specifically aimed at acquiring this type of animal-centred information is to use preference or choice tests as a way of telling us how an animal views the world. By giving an animal the opportunity to choose between two different environments, or to press a lever in order to gain access to or escape from something, we gain some insight into the animal's world.

Preference tests provide the clearest picture of how an animal, as opposed to a well-meaning human onlooker, views the world and even more importantly, hold out the possibility of enabling us to be objective about a concept that has been as elusive as it has been popularly used – the concept of an ethological 'need' (Dawkins, 1983).

Certain objections may be raised to preference tests. Most farm animals are reared in environments which are very different from those of their wild or feral counterparts. Can these animals suffer through the absence of something they never had? Has its unnatural environment turned it effectively into a different sort of animal whose welfare should be evaluated differently? A further objection is that preference tests may give misleading results, as experience early in life does make a substantial difference to later preferences of the adult animal.

There are two points to be made about these objections. Firstly, early experience can affect many different aspects of an animal's biology, not just its preferences. Its response to its environment, such as the amount of escape behaviour and the physiological changes which accompany this, may be strongly affected by what it has experienced before.

The second is that the last objection is not, strictly speaking, an objection at all. Whether the preferences we are testing are or are not affected by early experience is an empirical point, and something we have to do an experiment to find out. It may turn out that early experience has relatively little effect, in which case we need not worry about it. Or, it may turn out to have a major effect, in which case we have to specify, for any given preference, what sort of an upbringing the animal has had.

The following is an example quoted by Dawkins (1983). Two groups of similar hens were reared to 17 weeks of age – one on deep litter and the other in battery cages with a wire floor. The hens were given preference tests to see how they responded to four different cages, a large cage (0.76 × 0.86m) with a litter floor, a large cage with a wire floor, a small cage (0.38 × 0.43 m) with a litter floor, and a small cage with a wire floor. There was an overall preference for the large cages over the small ones, showing that space is important. There was also a preference for litter floors over wire ones, even among the hens that had never before been exposed to litter during the whole of their lives. In other words, a bird did not need to be reared on litter in order to show a preference for it and the previous experience of the bird appeared to have little effect. The preference for litter appears to be *robust* in the face of varying rearing conditions.

Thus the objections made to the preference tests that they are highly sensitive to the condition in which animals have been used can be met by doing experiments to see whether or not this is the case. It may turn out that early experience makes little apparent difference, as in the case of the litter preference of hens; or it may be that it makes a lot of difference, in which case we would not be entitled to make general statements about all members of a species. In fact, other measures of welfare may also be dependent on early environment.

A fourth objection is related to genetics and suggests that different genetic strains within one species may have varying preferences or make different choices. The objection can be met quite simply by doing experiments to find out whether this is true or not.

The fifth objection is that preference tests are highly sensitive to the particular conditions in which the test is carried out. This is also true but can be dealt with by appropriate planning of the experiment.

Another objection is that preference tests are no good because animals do not always choose what is best for their health. This can be dealt with by ensuring that other factors are taken into account.

Yet another objection is that 'preference doesn't mean suffering' – just because an animal prefers one thing to another or chooses one set of conditions over another, this cannot be taken to mean that it necessarily suffers if it has to make do with its least preferred state. In other words, a lack of preference for something does not mean suffering.

Similar difficulties beset other measures of welfare. For example, we may detect some physiological change in an animal, a change in its heart rate, brain state or hormonal levels, but it cannot immediately be concluded that the animal is suffering. The animal may be showing a perfectly normal response to a slight change in its environment. The problem of the degree of reaction, whether it is a physiological measure, a behavioural measure, a preference or whatever, is one which besets all measures of welfare. What is required is a way of calibrating the various signs of welfare and suffering in a quantitative way of distinguishing high levels of frustration, fear and other unpleasant emotional states from mild or momentary discomfort or alertness that we would not want to call suffering.

Everyone agrees that animals suffer if kept without food. If the animals tell us that some other commodity, such as litter to scratch and dust-bathe in, is as important to them, as shown by the fact that they are willing to give up feeding time to obtain it, then that commodity, too, must be counted as a necessity. We ask the animals not merely what they like but how much it is worth to them in terms of something known to be essential. We ask them whether they have a *need* for it – whether they regard access to something as a luxury or a necessity. Thus does Dr. Dawkins argue very effectively the value of the preference test in building up the knowledge on which we can base the proposed Welfare Index.

A classification of the welfare hazards in modern husbandry

As we have seen, modern husbandry systems can seriously

disrupt behaviour and reduce welfare both through the physical environment and through their effects on the social environment. A classification scheme for these effects has been given by Duncan (1983) and his comments on these follow.

First, some aspect of the environment may block or frustrate the tendency to perform a particular activity. Secondly, the environment may lack specific releasing stimuli which are necessary for eliciting certain behavioural units or fixed action patterns. Third, the level of general stimulation may be too high because the artificial environment is complex and changing or too low because it is barren or repetitive.

Frustration is the situation in which an animal is prevented, by some form of obstacle, from obtaining a goal, and it appears to be accepted that the state of frustration implies a reduction in welfare. However, it is not easy to decide what definitely constitutes frustration. It is simple in the case of the basic maintenance activities such as eating, drinking, some body-care and sleeping: if these are blocked, frustration will occur sooner or later. However, it is more difficult to decide in the case of certain aspects of sexual behaviour, parental behaviour, and exploratory behaviour.

The UK Welfare Recommendations suggest that an animal should have sufficient freedom of movement to turn round, groom itself, get up, lie down and stretch its limbs without difficulty. However, many management and housing systems do not allow this, for example, systems which tether animals, prevent them from turning round, and this includes many traditional systems as well as modern ones. Also, crates for farrowing sows and veal calves do not allow all these freedoms. Perhaps any housing system which involves severe confinement will be potentially frustrating?

It has long been suggested that artificial, intensive housing systems frustrate particular fixed action patterns. For example, keeping hens in cages will frustrate ground-scratching and dust-bathing; keeping pigs on bare concrete floors will frustrate rooting, and keeping cattle in slatted yards will frustrate grazing. This is where the debate starts in earnest. Does a hen *need* to dust-bathe, or a pig *need* to root or a cow *need* to graze? Do animals have behavioural needs? If put in a varied and stimulating environment, all of our domestic species have shown incredibly rich ethograms. They have the potential to show many and varied action patterns (Duncan, 1983).

Lack of specific releasing stimuli

In some circumstances, a behavioural tendency is not released because the specific releasing stimulus is absent. An example is the case of hens of certain strains which do not show normal sitting behaviour before laying in battery cages. As another example, the lack of key stimuli often leads to difficulty in feeding behaviour in early weaned animals, particularly the calf and pig.

Incorrect general stimulation

It is suggested that animals will always try to maintain an optimal level of sensory input (Hebb, 1955; Leuba, 1955). An animal can increase its sensory input by exploring its environment and reduce it by performing certain behavioural patterns or adopting certain postures which tend to cut off the arousing stimuli. In a confined and barren environment there is a limit to the amount of exploration an animal can do. Whether or not this will lead to what man calls boredom is debatable. There is little experimental evidence to answer this argument.

Social environment

Modern husbandry systems can disrupt the social environment in very many ways. For example, cages tend to keep animals in small groups, and dairy systems tend to keep animals in a single-sex group.

Intensive husbandry systems often deviate from 'natural' systems in the following ways:

1. The formation of the normal parent-offspring bond may be disrupted or prevented completely. For example, artificially reared chicks have no contact with their dams or with a substitute dam, and in most dairying systems the calf is removed from its dam soon after birth.
2. Young animals may be weaned early, e.g. piglets.
3. Animals may be kept in large or small groups, e.g. broilers in tens of thousands, egg layers in small numbers.
4. Animals may be kept at a high density, e.g. cattle in yards, pigs in pens, broiler chicken on deep litter and hens in cages.
5. Animals tend to be kept in single age groups, e.g. in fattening pigs and broilers, or dairy cows.

6. Group membership may be disrupted, e.g. dry cows are removed, newly calved cows are returned to the herd.
7. Animals may be isolated, e.g. boars and bulls away from the herd.

However, as yet there is little evidence that these procedures are harmful to the animals' welfare.

References

Baxter, M.R. (1983) 'Housing and welfare from first principles.' in *Farm Animal Housing and Welfare* pp. 3–7. The Hague: Martinus Nijhoff.

Cannon, W.B. (1935) 'Stresses and strains of homeostasis.' *Amer. J. Med. Sci.*, **189** 1.

Dantzer, R., Mormède, P. and Henry, J.P. (1983) 'Physiological assessment of adaptation in farm animals.' in *Farm Animal Housing and Welfare* pp. 8–19. The Hague: Martinus Nijhoff.

Dawkins, M. (1980) *Animal Suffering: The Science of Animal Welfare.* London: Chapman & Hall.

Duncan, I.J.H. (1983) 'Assessing the effect of housing on welfare.' in *Farm Animal Housing and Welfare* pp. 27–35. The Hague: Martinus Nijhoff.

Hebb, D.O. (1955) 'Drives and C.N.S.' *Psychological Review*, **62**, 243–354.

Henry, J.P. and Stephens, P.M. (1977) 'Stress, health and the social environment.' in *A Sociobiologic Approach to Medicine.* New York: Springer Verlag.

Leuba, C. (1955) 'Toward some integration of learning theories: the concept of optimal stimulation.' *Psychol. Report*, **1** 27–33.

Selye, H. (1936) 'A syndrome produced by diverse nocuous agents.' *Nature* **138** 32.

12 Welfare and the Pig

General introduction

The pig is a superbly interesting animal. It is inquisitive, intelligent and highly responsive to its environment and conditions of housing. The pig is the only animal on the farm which naturally endeavours to maintain clean habits and, if the facilities are right, will dung and urinate away from its lying area, which it endeavours to keep clean. In fact we may consider the housing system we provide for the pigs has failed if they are unable to keep clean and they foul the area they lie on.

For many hundreds of years the 'traditional' system for housing domestic pigs was the 'cottager's pigsty', a small kennel for a sow and litter or a group of growing pigs, with an outside yard for dunging, exercise, feeding and drinking. Such a system is healthy and provides generous space, but cleaning is laborious and the lack of control of the environmental conditions can lead to uneven growth and poor efficiency of conversion of the pig's food to flesh. Many developments since then have led to a multitude of alternative systems which we shall consider in this chapter.

In general, the most common design of piggery nowadays gives pigs a lying area on a solid floor and a separate dunging area which may be solid or perforated. In most cases these layouts are enclosed in well-insulated buildings and ventilation is more often by mechanical means since there are frequently large numbers and a high concentration of pigs in these forms of accommodation, which makes a positive fan-assisted air flow necessary. Nevertheless, health and other problems do quite often develop in high-density stocking buildings such as this. They may be diseases, such as swine dysentery or enzootic pneumonia, or behavioural problems such as tail-biting or other more serious forms of cannibalism. Major difficulties also

Plate 1 Interior of piggery with solid floors and liquid feeding

develop where the pigs insist on dunging in the lying area, due usually to defects in the environment. In this case the labour in cleaning is vastly and often impossibly increased; the pigs are seriously contaminated with their own excreta and there can also be serious contamination of their feed and water. Where bedding cannot be used – or at least where it is very difficult or uneconomic to do so – one answer that has been used for many years is the perforated or slatted floor over the whole pen. Such a device is described elsewhere but it is an expensive system and only works well if the pen size is small. Such a sophisticated arrangement also usually requires a positive pressure ventilation arrangement and the highest standard of thermal insulation, as the pigs are unprotected by bedding or even a warm floor surface, and thus the air temperature must be higher to compensate for these factors.

In order to avoid all the complexities associated with these arrangements used in totally enclosed buildings, there is a growing enthusiasm for developments based on the old cottager's pigsty, retaining its attributes of small groups, spaciousness for the pigs and separate lying and exercising areas. There are numerous types of building to cater for this requirement, suited to virtually any climate in the world. Some place kennels in covered yards so the 'outside' facilities are still protected, and this is ideal for temperate or cool areas. In other cases the kennel is the only protected part and the yards where feeding and dunging take place are outside. This is ideal for areas with a mild climate, and is the cheapest of all forms of housing. Careful design reduces any stress on the pigs. Perhaps the most popular arrangement is the widely advocated monopitch house with open front and sharply sloping roof to a protected and cosy area in the rear. This is a system which is ideally suited to the belief that it is best to allow the animal the space for choice; in summer the pig moves to the front for sun and fresh air, and in the winter to the back for warmth. Dunging and feeding are in the more open part and there are many alternative arrangements possible for easy servicing and dung cleaning.

Farrowing accommodation

Full details of the climatic requirements of the sow and piglet have been given in Chapter 4 and it has been emphasised that the modern sow as we have bred her tends to be a clumsy mother, so that a protective crate or other device is considered essential to prevent her cumbersome movements crushing the piglets. At the same time, the piglets must be encouraged to spend their resting periods away from the immediate proximity of the sow, and this is best done by providing nests close to the crate or as part of the crate itself. Ideally, artificial heat and light sources should be placed above or around the nest to attract and warm the piglets. Also, the pigman must keep a watchful eye on the sow and piglets over the farrowing period and it is therefore essential to provide easy inspecting facilities.

For all these reasons the totally enclosed, specialised farrowing house is preferred. Nevertheless, every farmer should be aware of the fatal error of making the house too big. Sows and piglets need hygienic surroundings, which means that an essential requirement is periodic depopulation and disinfection of the building. Sows also need quiet surroundings and they get this much more easily in the smaller building. The aim is to have a unit of a maximum of 16–20 pens within a building, and preferably less. But the limiting factor is that it must be small enough to be emptied of all stock regularly.

Plate 2 Farrowing pen with metal alloy flooring

The farrowing crate unit

The simplest farrowing crate consists of a pair of three parallel rails. The top rails are set 530 mm apart, as also are the centre rails. The bottom rails are 750–800 mm apart, depending on the type of sow, to allow adequate room where she lies down. The bottom rails are a minimum of 250 mm from the floor and the second row is 300 mm above the bottom row and 300 mm below the top. Thus the crate has a total height of 850 mm from the floor. There are escape nests on each side, a minimum of 530 mm wide. Thus the total width of the crate is 1.6–1.65 m, or with dividing walls approximately 1.8 m. The walls at the outside of the nests and at the front of the crate can be solid, and there is a gate at the back for access by the sow and the attendant. On the inside of this gate there should be a semi-circular metal bar 250 mm from the base extending 230 mm inside the gate. This will prevent the sow backing right up against the gate and crushing the piglets. In many crates the position of the bottom rail is adjustable to allow for variations in

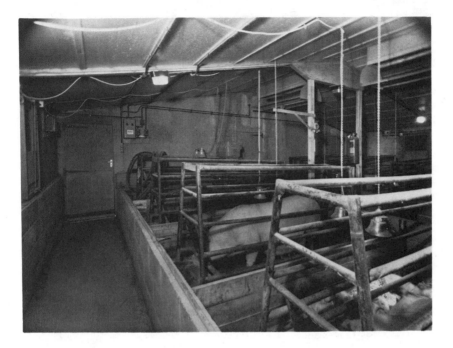

Plate 3 Interior of typical farrowing house with crates

height and width, depending on the size of the sow. There are many proprietary crates on the market with their own unique features and the final choice made by the farmer is very much a case of individual preference.

It is desirable to have a cover of plywood, hardboard or asbestos sheet over each nest to conserve heat and reduce floor draughts, and also a heat source, either an electric infra-red lamp or a gas heater. Great care must be taken with the falls in the floor to make sure that any water or urine runs towards the back and away from the crate and the creep. There are also so-called 'blow-away' units, which are designed around the observation that piglets dislike cold draughts. When the sow is standing, the unit, which is fitted to the side of the farrowing crate, blows cold air under the sow. This creates a draught which the piglets find uncomfortable to lie in. The cool air blower is triggered by the sow breaking an infra-red beam across the farrowing crate when she stands. On lying down, she gets out of the path of the beam and the draught stops. This allows the piglets to suckle in comfort. Being portable, the unit is

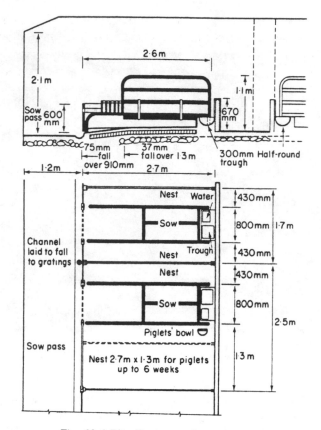

Fig. 12.1 Pitmillan-type farrowing pen

moved from crate to crate soon after farrowing; usually 72 hours after is sufficient.

As sows vary in size, the gate at the back of the crate is sometimes made to fit in a number of runners situated at distances measuring from the front 2.3 m, 2.2 m and 2.1 m. Another refinement is to have several metal bars across the top of the crate to prevent the sow rearing up. This fitting is best left portable so that the bars can be used as and when required.

The most popular type of farrowing units are based on the Ritchie farrowing crates in Pitmillan-type pens (Fig 12.1). These are fixed crates with creep areas on each side with low walls allowing easy access to the piglets. The nests are 430 mm wide on each side if the piglets are removed early before there is feeding in the creep, or if the latter is to take place, the creep on one side is increased to 1.3 m. Sows and litters may be kept in this accommodation up to 6 weeks after farrowing. It should also be mentioned that some farmers prefer the piglet creep to be in front of the sow; this has the merit of encouraging the piglets to an even safer position and also making inspection and handling easier.

All the measures referred to in the foregoing paragraphs are concerned with protecting the piglets from crushing, cold, wet or generally unhealthy conditions. The crate for the sow is, however, restrictive to her movements and very careful examination is currently being undertaken by both Professor Wood-Gush at Edinburgh University and Dr. Baxter at the Farm Buildings Investigation Unit at Aberdeen to establish exactly what a sow and her piglets require in order to provide them with optimal conditions for productivity, health and welfare. It seems likely that from this work may emerge new concepts, orientated very much towards the needs of the pigs as well as the farmer, but until this work is completed the farrowing crate in its various existing forms remains as a satisfactory arrangement.

Slatted-floor farrowing pens

There has more recently been a considerable following for farrowing pens with either part-slatted (perforated) or entirely slatted (perforated) flooring.

In the case of the latter a suitable slat has been either a 75 mm or 100 mm concrete one with a normal gap of 12–20 mm but with an enlarged gap of 20–28 mm in a 0.18 m^2 area behind the sow. For the first week after farrowing, the area behind the sow is covered with expanded metal to prevent the baby pigs catching their feet in the gap.

Two forms of part-slatted pens have been tried with success. In one case 75 mm slats have been used with 12 mm gaps and only the rear half of the pens is slatted. In another case a similar area is used but the slats are of expanded metal, 44 mm long and 12 mm across, with the grid supported every 25 mm by metal cross-pieces. It is best to use galvanised metal. Those who have used this system have established the importance of keeping the piglets, and indeed the sow, warm since there is no bedding, or at the most only a modest amount for the piglets in the early stages. It is also especially important that the slats, if concrete is used, should be impeccably finished, otherwise both the sows and the piglets will suffer. The most recent innovation for slatted floors is to use panels of polypropylene plastic which give a very 'kind' surface finish for the pigs.

One very useful method of satisfying the requirement for a slatted floor farrowing arrangement consists of a raised and portable platform farrowing unit on tubular steel legs. The floor is perforated except for a recessed mat 20 mm thick and 1 m square under the sow's udder and with boarding in the creep box which is placed in front of the sow.

It may well be questioned whether from the welfare angle it is acceptable to have totally slatted floors at all for sows and piglets. On the basis of the experimental evidence given elsewhere in this book, and knowing of the dangers of injury, disease and discomfort, it may be argued that there should always be some area of solid floor and a provision of some bedding and straw.

The Solari farrowing pen

A simpler approach to the farrowing and rearing of pigs is epitomised in a design that aims to keep litters warm and comfortable by providing a limited air-space and freedom from draughts, and keep the sow's movements under control by the judicious use of farrowing rails and a limited area for the pens.

The pens in the 'Solari house' consist of a range of units each 1.5 m wide and 4.95 m long. The height at the back of the pen is 910 mm, rising to 2.4 m at the front. In the front there is only a wall and a door, both 1.2 m high, leaving a 1.2 m high open area above to allow free air circulation. There is a creep of 750 mm depth the whole way across the back, formed by a simple steel grille. Farrowing rails are fitted extending 1.75 m in front of the creeps and there is a space of 830 mm between them, and the sow lies voluntarily in this area. This leaves the rest of the pen for exercising, feeding and dunging.

Only the rear part of the pen floor is insulated, to encourage the sow to lie in this area and there is a good fall from back to front of 130 mm. The farrowing rails are 150 mm from the floor while the side ones are 250 mm. All the equipment is easily demountable: when the pen is used for farrowing, all the equipment will be in place; after 10 days the rails will be removed, leaving only the creep grille. Should it be desired to continue using the pen thereafter, the creep also may be removed.

Adaptation for porkers

An adaptation of this pen for use from birth to finishing is to place a slatted or weld-mesh area in the front which is covered during the farrowing and rearing stage but uncovered afterwards when the sow is removed. A pen can take up to 20 porkers, so use of this accommodation is extremely economical.

Its disadvantages are that environmental controls are incomplete and labour requirements are quite heavy. Inspection and access are more difficult than in the totally enclosed house, the pigman has no protection while tending the pigs and the nest and creep are behind the sow and therefore more difficult to reach. Nevertheless, any system which leaves the piglet in the same accommodation, without the stress of moving and mixing, clearly has much to commend it from welfare aspects.

Farrowing outdoors

The easiest farrowing accommodation to manage is certainly the indoor, totally enclosed unit, but the merits of outdoor farrowing are not inconsiderable. In general, outdoor units are healthier, due to the isolation, and they are also much cheaper in capital costs, although maintenance can be high.

A hard-wearing unit for outdoor farrowing is the 'ark' shape. The Craibstone ark, designed by the Farm Buildings Department of the North of Scotland College of Agriculture, is an excellent example (Fig. 12.2). Dimensions are 2.4 m long, 2.1 m wide and 1.5 m high. The shape of the hut itself forms an escape for the piglets where the roof meets the floor and it is also a shape that makes for economy and rigidity. Some of the essential features of outdoor farrowing huts, of which several types exist, are well shown in this hut but should be incorporated in any farrowing unit.

The first essential is sound, two-skin construction which ensures warmth and freedom from draughts. Next, really good baffling is placed inside the door to deflect wind from the nest. All huts must incorporate a nest and creep feeding and watering

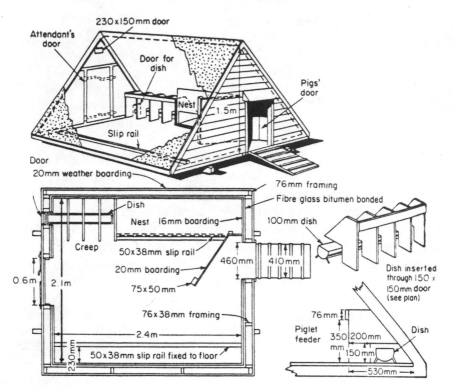

Fig. 12.2 The Craibstone ark. An excellent design for outdoor rearing

arrangements when the building is to be used for rearing. To keep the piglets warm in their nest, straw is packed on top of it or artificial heating is commonly provided by the use of portable gas heaters.

Access to the sow and litter is by a door at the back, 600 mm wide at least, and extending 1.05 m high. The door must be extremely tight fitting, to give a complete seal when closed (see Fig. 12.2). In the Craibstone ark there is also a small observation door up to 300 mm square in the back that is used for quiet inspection without disturbing the sow. It is usual to fit wooden battens to the floor 50 mm wide and 37 mm deep along the sides, 230 mm from the edge, to prevent the sow's feet jamming the piglets against the wall and causing them injury.

Rectangular hut with creep

Another common type of farrowing hut is of rectangular shape and measures 2.4 m long and 1.65 m wide, plus a further 600 mm extension at the back to form the special creep. The height at the front is 1.2 m and at the back 910 mm. As well as baffle doorways, creeps and nests, there must also be a farrowing rail 250 mm from the floor and 250 mm from the wall. With both farrowing huts and ark there may be a fold unit in front, usually about 3.6 m long, or the sows may run in paddocks or very occasionally are tethered. To inspect the pigs the roof may be constructed to be raised or may slide open.

There are also some circular farrowing huts with central creeps and nests which have been popular, especially in New Zealand, for many years.

Whichever type of accommodation is used, farmers practising this type of outdoor husbandry have reported excellent results when great care is taken with the details of management. Pigs must be regularly moved to prevent the land becoming 'pig-sick' – that is, excessively contaminated with pathogenic parasites and bacteria. Climatic stresses such as excessive heat or cold, or wet and snow, put a strain on the attendant which needs to be planned for. Capital costs are low and benefits to poor, light land can be considerable from the pigs' muck, but dedicated labour is required. It is, however, encouraging to report that many pigmen prefer the more open-air life to the possibly less healthy and invigorating environment of the enclosed piggery.

Multi-suckling pens

One of the major problems of pig husbandry is the serious check that takes place when piglets are weaned and mixed at the same time. One approach is the farrow-to-finish pen where pigs are taken from birth to finishing in the same pen. Another, known as the multi-suckling pen, is to mix 3–5 sows and litters together, usually at about 3 weeks of age, and thereby form a 'weaner pool' which includes the dams. After about two weeks the sows are removed and the group of 30–50 weaners is left for a further period, nearly always ad lib feeding until ready for the finishing stages of fattening.

There is no doubt that weaners mix much better if they are

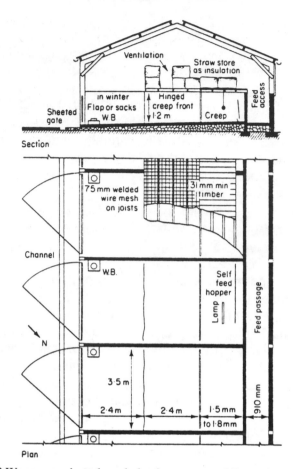

Fig. 12.3 Weaner pools and yards for four sows and litters (floor-fed sow cobs)

still receiving their mother's milk. Considerable flexibility is possible with the housing which may be totally enclosed or yarded, and a proven example is shown in Fig. 12.3. The essentials are as follows. Adequate space, at least 6 m² for each sow and litter. Plenty of bedding is preferable under most systems and a large creep for the piglets of not less than 0.2 m² per piglet gives plenty of food and water space. The creep should also be warmed and covered in the usual way. Individual feeders for the sows are recommended wherever possible, but they are such a costly item that they may have to be dispensed with. The design can be tractor cleaned. At present the multi-suckling system is less popular in the pig industry in general but continues to be practised by a large number of enthusiasts in many areas of the world, who appreciate the intrinsic merits of the system.

The 'early weaner'

One of the most difficult welfare problems is the accommodation required for the early-weaned pig. Probably the 'natural' age for the weaning of pigs would be about 8 weeks, by which time the sow is 'dry' and the piglets have changed more or less entirely to solid food and water. Early weaning as it is now practised is done at about 3 weeks of age and has some advantages in the growth of the young pigs but most of all in the better rate of breeding from the sow, lifting the number of litters per annum from under 2 to about 2.4.

Early weaning was first practised in the early 1950s and, to start with, was very successful. The nutritional needs had been successfully elucidated and the process appeared to be an ideal one for piglet rearing. However, within a very short time virulent infections tended to emerge and the systems were generally abandoned at this time as the industry had no answer to the disease problems. However, a few years later a successful arrangement was produced which placed the piglets in simple strawbale huts outdoors on pasture – so-called outdoor early weaning. From the husbandry point of view it was most successful; the warm huts for fairly small groups of 10–20 piglets were used only for a short period of a few litters before they were abandoned and new units erected on clean pasture. Thus the 'build-up' of infection was eliminated. However, for management reasons, the system did not become established on any scale; it was labour-intensive, and bad weather conditions, though of no harm to the piglets in their cosy accommodation, made the servicing of the piglets very time-consuming.

From here emerged the next system, which remains as a most effective one, and this is the 'kennel and run', the run in this case nearly always having some form of slatted floor, whilst the kennel has a solid floor, often of wood for warmth and ease of construction. Several forms of these kennels have been used: there is the very simple outdoor raised kennel and run, healthy for the piglets but not too popular due to servicing difficulties, and, very much more popular, the row of kennels covered over

for the stockman's benefit but in a freely-ventilated shed. Single-
or double-sided units are used, the former being much better
since the disposition of the open yard can be more favourably
arranged. These are shown in Fig. 12.4.

The third and possibly the most popular of all arrangements is
the 'flat-deck', which is often stated to be a welfare risk for the
piglets. The 'flat-deck' is a totally perforated floor unit in a
controlled environment, windowless house with artificial heating. There are a considerable number of management advantages of this arrangement. Environmental conditions are maintained at a suitable level of temperature and ventilation.
Inspection and servicing of the piglets is straightforward and
health should be easily maintained. Pens are usually small to
take roughly a litter-group size and good hygiene can quite
easily be maintained. The crux of the system, to some extent, is
the type of flooring used. It is difficult for the flat-deck to
function satisfactorily without a totally perforated floor since
enteric infections easily emerge with solid areas. Certainly great
efforts have been made to produce good, comfortable perforated flooring; good forms are perforated metal, plastic-covered
wire of various forms and polypropylene all-plastic flooring.

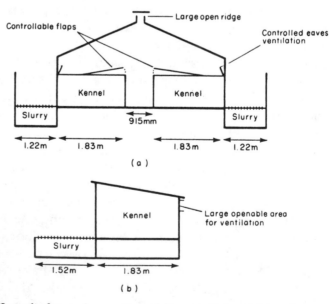

Fig. 12.4 Kennels for early weaning: (a) covered kennel housing, natural
ventilation, (b) outside kennels, natural ventilation

With early weaning there is another and totally different approach which is still practised successfully in some localities. In this case the piglets are weaned at the same times as in other early weaning arrangements, that is, at about 21 days, and are placed in deep straw bedded yards, with some form of kennel at the back to keep them warm. The secret of success with this system is to provide a very great depth of straw so it is always available for them to busy themselves in when the climate dictates. The diluting effect of abundant straw removes the risk of infection and at the same time gives excellent natural environmental control. A real advantage of this system is that it is one of great simplicity, can be practised under almost any cover, and produces good manure from straw in a system which combines good welfare and conservation with good husbandry and results. Plenty of space is essential – about 1 m^2 per piglet. It is very satisfactory if it is carried out in a seasonal way, if so desired, so that the building is rested a good deal between batches, or there may even be other livestock put through from time to time.

All systems, if properly designed and managed, are capable of giving equally good results. An interesting study was carried out at the National Agriculture Centre at Stoneleigh, Warwickshire in 1979 (Table 12.1) which compared fully slatted flat-decks with simpler kennels and verandahs either with slatted floor runs or solid floor runs. It will be noted there was next to nothing in the physical results to choose between the three systems.

Table 12.1 Food conversion rate and mortality compared for flat-decks, and first-stage kennels (from the National Agricultural Centre, Stoneleigh, Warwickshire, 1979)

	Flat-decks	First-stage kennels slatted runs	First-stage kennels solid runs
Food convertion efficiency	1.5	1.5	1.5
Mortality	1.1	1.6	0.6

Their conclusion: 'A comparison between the results for the flat-deck and kennel systems shows a remarkable similarity in terms of physical performance. It demonstrates that two completely different systems of weaning at 3 weeks can work equally well, given good levels of stockmanship'.

The main early weaning systems

The kennel system

There is a choice between two arrangements – either the kennel and outdoor verandah, or the all-indoor (see Fig. 12.4). The former has a solid bed and usually a perforated floor for the verandah. The kennel and verandah was the first system developed, and represented a major breakthrough, since it is a technique which gives reasonably consistent results. Its advantages are considerable: low cost housing; isolation between small groups; warmth without artificial heating and ventilation; good muck disposal from the pigs, ensuring the essential criterion of separation of pigs and muck. Nevertheless, the system has disadvantages. In order to ensure warmth the piglets do need to be penned closely; if this is in any way done excessively it can lead to uneven growth and difficult inspection. The variation in the environment between the different seasons, which is inevitable in housing like this, means that careful and individual care of the kennels is required.

Perhaps the most important feature to emphasise is the need to be able to control ventilation adequately in all kennel arrangements. With the outdoor kennel there must be ventilators at the rear to give controlled air flow, especially in the hot weather, while for the kennel placed inside a covered yard, not only should there be ventilation from top flaps on the kennel, but the house itself should also be well ventilated.

A critical factor in the successful rearing of pigs from 3 weeks onwards is achieving the correct balance between the numbers in the group and the space they are allowed. Many trials have been conducted on pigs of all ages and in summary they have shown:

1. over-stocking retards growth;
2. small groups do better than large ones; and
3. the litter group is the ideal.

Therefore if the benefits that are undoubtedly obtainable by 3-week weaning are to be realised, it is essential that the very large groups which are often seen should be avoided. Indeed, they form probably the most frequent basis of criticism of such housing. This is especially common in the kennel arrangement since it is here that there is an in-built temptation to crowd the pigs in large groups in low-roofed kennels to ensure a high temperature. For example, it is not uncommon to have 50 piglets in one pen, but the troubles this can produce range from uneven growth, poor food conversion and vices such as tail-biting, to scour, pneumonia and rhinitis.

In general, while a small group is ideal and often obtainable with flat-decks, a group of up to 25 seems perfectly acceptable, with the absolute necessity, where large numbers are used, of providing rather more space to compensate. The optimum total floor area should be approximately 10 kg live-weight of pig to each 0.1 m^2 of floor space. If the flooring is partly solid and partly perforated, then the living area may be reduced by about 25%, but an extra area for dunging must be added on top of this.

The 'flat-deck' house

The relative simplicity of the 'flat-deck' totally perforated floor has much to commend it since it can ensure a completely clean floor (Fig. 12.5). There are four main types of flooring so used. Punch-perforated steel floors with a very smooth finish are costly but kind on the pig's feet and can be long-lasting. A cheaper flooring is expanded metal.

The welded mesh floor has the biggest area of void and is probably the cleanest, but can be the least comfortable and most damaging, whereas the perforated steel floor has the largest solid area, may be a little dirtier, but is usually the most comfortable. In all cases galvanising of the steel has the advantage that it greatly increases the life of the metal floor, which would otherwise not last many years. The latest material used for floors is polypropylene plastic and this is proving most successful so far.

A trough space of 100 mm per pig is sufficient, with one drinker per 10 pigs. Whilst nipple drinkers are perfectly satisfactory, it is an added advantage if, for the first few days, there is a water trough with more accessible water.

There are some doubts on the question of light. It is usual practice to keep the piglets in fairly dim lighting conditions in order to reduce their activity and only raise the lights for

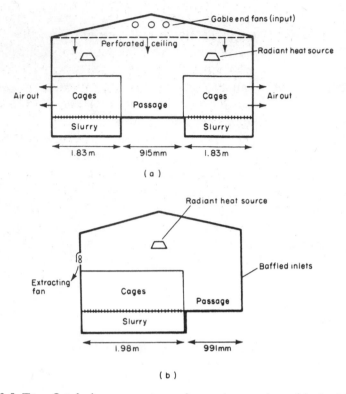

Fig. 12.5 Two flat-deck cage systems for early weaning: (a) double row pressurised, (b) single row extraction

inspection. In fact animals kept in dim conditions usually adapt themselves quite well to them and it is difficult to see any welfare hazard involved.

Cage rearing

A few pig farmers rear piglets away from the sow from about 7 days of age. Piglets are grouped by weight, nine at a time, in cages three, four or five tiers high. Each cage measures 1 200 m long × 600 mm wide and 390 mm high and has a floor of 12 mm × 12 mm × 12 gauge wire mesh or plastic. Such cages are placed in housing kept at 27°C and in subdued light. The piglets remain here until about 7 kg weight, after which they are usually moved to flat-deck cages.

From the welfare aspect this system may be seriously criticised. The piglets are not easy to inspect or handle and

Plate 4 'Flat-deck' pig pen with metal alloy slates

frequently suck each other, to the detriment of their health and growth. The environment is barren as well as dark and the piglets usually appear restless and unsettled.

Fattening accommodation

The totally enclosed house

While there are several fundamentally different forms of piggery for the fattening stages in the pig's life, probably overall the most popular is the totally enclosed piggery, where the environment is under complete control and all attendance to the pigs is carried out under cover. A basis of design and the most familiar world-wide is the Danish-style layout (Fig. 12.6). It consists of a central feeding passage 1.2 m wide, side dunging passages 1.05 m and a pen of 3 × 1.8 m to hold 10–12 pigs to bacon weight. This conventional arrangement is probably the most expensive of all designs in layout and cubic area per pig, but it remains an adaptable design and is particularly suitable for

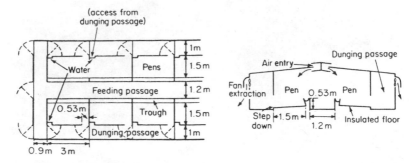

Fig. 12.6 Danish-type fattening house with screened-off dunging passage

the small pig keeper. It has the advantage that the pigs are kept in small groups and management can be of a high standard. Feeding is simple and can be carried out easily with a trolley or overhead conveyor; dung cleaning may be by hand or squeegee, or by mechanical means. Straw may or may not be used, as desired. It is advisable to screen off the dunging passage from the pens, leaving only a pop-hole between the pen and the passage. This greatly improves environmental control, as the pigs in effect lie in a building within a building. In such a design, making use of good insulation and with mechanical ventilation taking in fresh air from the ridge, temperatures within the range 20–25°C may readily be maintained. Only the central part of the house needs complete insulation. It is always best to place a number of complete partitions across a Danish-type piggery and aim to have not more than 200 pigs within a common air-space, and 800–1 000 pigs in one building.

Wide-span totally enclosed house

In an important attempt to produce a more economical piggery, though of the same basic layout, and where trough feeding is required, a wider-span building may be employed by running the troughs between the pens. In the Danish layout the cross-section is approximately 7.9 m, 2.1 m being taken up by the dunging passage, 3.9 m by the pens and trough and 1.2 m by the feeding passage, with the walls making up the total of 7.9 m. If, however, a wider span of 13.3 m is used, the dunging passages may each be 1.5 m, making 3 m in all, the central service passage may be 1.2 m and the pen depth may be 4–5 m on each

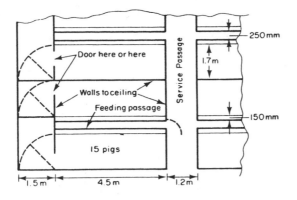

Fig. 12.7 Fattening house suitable for large unit, built as single- or double-sided unit

side to take 15 pigs to bacon weight. The depth of the pen behind the trough may be 1.7 m, the trough 300 mm and the catwalk serving the trough 300 mm. Such a design is shown in Fig. 12.7. The economy of this design is apparent when it is noted that whereas 6 pigs can be kept in each metre length of a Danish house, in each metre of this type the number of pigs can be double. When automatic floor feeding systems are used, no trough is needed, and with any automatic feeding systems the catwalks between the pens may be omitted. The extra space will allow for 1–2 extra pigs per pen. A popular modification is to make the dunging passage 2.1 m wide to allow tractor cleaning.

Central dunging passage

In order to reduce labour or activities associated with dung cleaning, an improvement on the traditional design is the installation of one central dunging passage, rather than a centre feeding passage, which allows access by the pigs from each pen to half the length of the passage opposite their pen (Fig. 12.8).

Ventilation can be quite simply by extraction of stale air over the dunging passage. It is noteworthy that the pigs have no contact at all with the outside walls of the house; this is quite an important point as the floors may well be warmer, much heat being lost laterally from the pig when it lies against the outside wall of a building. Nowadays, too, it has some constructional advantages, as many houses will be made out of prefabricated design, and lighter and less robust walling can be used, although

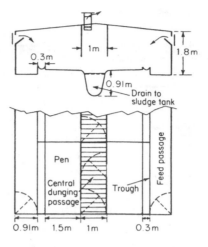

Fig. 12.8 House with centre dunging passage and side passage, using slatted floor

Plate 5 Exterior of piggery showing access at ends to solid floored dunging passage for tractor cleaning

it will, of course, be well insulated and vapour-sealed as in any other design. Also, with a centre passage there is considerable saving in cost; instead of two runs of dung passage there is only one, and the cost of this is little more than half, as the width need be increased only slightly.

Floor feeding with over-pen catwalk

This design has lent itself to further economies in building costs by the elimination of the side feeding passage. This is a very attractive proposition as it reduces the width of the buildings by over 2 m.

Feeding can be carried out by installing catwalks over the pens at the height of the pen division. A design of this type can be fitted into buildings of many shapes and sizes. For example, a single-sided unit could fit into a building as narrow as 3.6 m with a 1.05 m dunging passage and 2.4 × 2.7 m pens, taking 15 pigs to bacon weight.

Totally slatted floor

Pioneered in Scandinavia, the fattening piggery with totally slatted floors has a strong following. Although relatively expensive it is simple to manage and eliminates the major problem in slatted dung passage arrangements of persuading the pigs to dung in the right place.

Both of the two foregoing systems concentrate pigs within a building to such an extent that results in terms of productivity, and especially health, are sometimes disappointing. As little or no bedding can be used, there are further inherent welfare and husbandry risks. Hence they should only be used if the farmer is absolutely certain he has done everything possible to guard against all the risks involved.

Stocking densities

An important question in the design of fattening accommodation is how many pigs should be penned together. The evidence is that groups of fatteners are best in groups of not more than 15–20, with perhaps 10 as the ideal.

It is essential that when pigs are lying in the pen they cover the floor comfortably, otherwise there is a considerable risk that dirty habits will develop and muck will be deposited in the pens. The problem arises as to how one can ensure this when a weaner will occupy only about 0.18 m^2 of floor space when recumbent, whereas a baconer occupies some 0.46 m^2, and a heavy pig 0.50–0.55 m^2. Several solutions can be offered.

One is to design a pen with a sliding front so that the area can be enlarged as the pigs grow. Another solution for baconers and 'heavies' is to have pens of two sizes, one for the growing stage from weaning to, say, 16 weeks, and the other size from 16 weeks (45 kg) to finishing. If it is desired to have 15 pigs to a pen, the area of the grower pen would be 2.4 × 1.8 m, and the finishing pens could be 3.6 × 1.8 m. This arrangement envisages ad lib floor feeding in the grower stage and floor feeding in the finishing stage. If troughs were inserted, only 12–13 pigs could be penned under this arrangement. For bacon production, two finishing pens would be needed for every grower pen.

Another arrangement is to have a weaner pool at approximately 6–8 weeks, in which young pigs are placed in fairly large pens, 20–30 to a unit. They can be allowed 0.18–0.27m^2 of lying area and are kept there until they reach 45–54 kg. At this stage the best 10 are taken off to the finishing pens, when they can be divided off into well-balanced groups. One such weaner pool pen may therefore serve three finishing pens.

It is likely that the mixing of several litters at weaning creates a 'stress' from which the pigs may take some time to recover under intensive conditions, and it is for this reason that the deeply bedded yard with warm kennel lying area is more popular, allowing up to 0.74 m^2 per pig. The same system can be used if multiple suckling is practised, but without the severe weaning stress of several changes at once.

When the pigs do muck in the pens, it is always a help to clean and disinfect the floor and then place a barrier across part of the pen so that when they are lying down they really do fill the available space. The great limitation on the shape of the pen is that, with pigs being trough-fed, 230–380 mm of linear space has to be allowed to each pig so that pens are usually long and narrow. With floor feeding, such limitations are removed and much more economical buildings and conversions can be made but, as mentioned previously, floor feeding is often unsuccessful up to about the age when pigs reach 45 kg liveweight.

Dung disposal: enclosed piggery

In the totally enclosed piggery there are various methods of dung disposal. With solid-floored passages, the construction is cheap and the dung may be disposed of in solid or semi-solid form. Bedding may be used or not, but frequent cleaning is advisable; it cannot be considered acceptable to allow a build-up of dung inside a totally enclosed piggery as the evaporation of moisture and ammonia will make the internal atmosphere very unpleasant and the effect on the building structure undesirable.

The traditional method for a Danish piggery with solid floor and side dunging passages is to clean out with a shovel and barrow and provide trapped drains to take off the excess fluid. With such a design the dung is in solid form and bedding is optional. This method of cleaning can be mechanised by using a small horticultural cultivator with blade attachment and by pushing the muck through from end to end. While this can be used with side dunging passages, it is easier still with the arrangement of a central dunging passage and pens on each side, as there is one movement only of the machine through the piggery.

An alternative is to have a solid floor dunging passage with a step down from pen to pasage of 75–100 mm, omitting the drains, but with a virtually flat floor so that the passage can be cleaned out with either a mechanical scraper or a squeegee that is made to fit exactly the width of the passage. This is used in piggeries with little or no bedding and produces an end product in slurry form that can be dealt with as a liquid.

The easiest arrangement for dung disposal is the slatted floor with a channel or slurry pit underneath. Apart from its virtually automatic nature it is also probably the most hygienic, as the dung and urine pass to the channel below and have no inter-pen contact. Clean pens, however, must be maintained and research has shown that pens approximately twice as deep as they are wide are most successful in helping to achieve this necessity. In addition there should be a slatted area at least 910 mm or more in depth and approximately 0.55 m^2 of uninterrupted floor area for each bacon pig. Finally, the house temperature should not exceed 21°C if possible.

The slurry may be allowed to accumulate under the slats and be pumped out periodically through drainpipes fitted at intervals and opening to the outside. The pipe must be fitted with a cap to prevent draught blowing into the pen from under the slats. (In calculating the volume of space required for slurry, an allowance should be made of approximately 0.08 m^3 of slurry per pig per week with whey feeding (which produces the maximum), down to 0.04–0.05 m^3 per pig per week with meal feeding.)

Alternatively, a drain may be placed under the slats to take the slurry to a tank at the end or ends of the building. This channel is usually 600 mm deep, 910 mm wide or less at the top, sloping to 300 mm across at the base, which may have a half-round glazed pipe. A fall of between 1:120 and 1:180 is required and should not go outside this range. At the end of the channel, where it enters the tank, a sluice-gate of metal in wood runners is provided so that the sludge may be periodically run off into the tank.

Some piggeries, however, do not provide a sluice-gate and the system seems to work just as effectively with slurry trickling slowly into the pit. The sludge in the tank can be dealt with in a number of ways. It may be pumped out from the collecting tank and distributed through an irrigation system, or it may be pumped into a vacuum tank and spread over the fields from this. For these two latter processes quite costly equipment is needed, and the cost of the tank is also considerable. Access to the fields must be maintained for much of the year. An alternative way of dealing with the effluent is to run it onto straw or deep litter from poultry broiler or laying houses and then spread it in the same way solid muck. This method commends itself to many farmers who are unable to deal with the sludge in liquid form, yet desire the benefit of the slatted-floor system in piggery management. The fall on a solid-floored dunging passage to the drain is 1:20 to 1:30.

Fattening piggeries with yards

Whilst the totally enclosed fattening house represents the most popular trend at present and provides designs of general application throughout the country, under some circumstances piggeries with outside or covered yards may be strongly advocated. The advantages of such designs are several. A 'yarded' piggery is cheaper; the section of the building which needs to be well insulated is of more modest proportions and so the cost of materials and erection can be reduced. Also, some will consider the environment obtained by such designs basically healthier, for the dung and urine are outside the warm part of the building. Ventilation measures can therefore be on simpler lines. The yard itself can be left uncovered but this arrangement

Plate 6 Tri-form concrete slats in fattening pens

is only suitable for areas where the climate is mild and frosts infrequent or less severe. Covered yards are best in all other locations.

The greatest problem with piggeries with outside yards is, therefore, how to keep them warm and free from draughts in the cold weather. For this reason the size of the individual unit within the building must be kept small and each unit must be completely separate from the other units to prevent through-draught. The siting and aspect of the building are also critical factors. Open yards should always be of southerly aspect. Good baffle arrangements between the yard and the pen are necessary, and if fans are used, though this is rare, a reverse-acting ventilation system which blows the air into the piggery and out through the pop-holes is desirable, to reduce the risk of floor draughts.

Single-sided yarded piggeries

We may take as our pattern of the yarded piggery a good design of a single-sided, deep straw piggery with covered yard and individual cleaning. The design consists of a service passage running along one side of the unit, the wall containing double-glazed dead lights. From this passageway are catwalks at right angles serving pens on each side, each one being 4.8 m in length and 1.8 m deep, assuming that a trough is used.

There must be doors along the service passage between each pair of pens to prevent draughts blowing in the pop-holes at one end and out at the other. This part of the building is well insulated and may be ventilated by installing a push-in ventilation system by a duct running in the angle between the roof and the north wall, with the fans at each end. An alternative is to place fans in the north wall and force air into the pens, with a baffle placed in front to protect the pigs from direct draught. The walls between each pair of pens are taken to the roof and may be load-bearing and support it.

The yard is separated from the pen by a cavity wall. A pop-hole not more than 750 mm wide and 1.05 m high allows access for the pigs. Above the pop-hole may be a half-heck door to make for easier access between the pen and the yard, facilitating such operations as the weighing of the pigs. A curtain and baffle arrangement is needed to prevent excessive wind blowing in to the pens.

Open yards (Fig. 12.9)

A simple range of pens leading to uncovered yards is often used for whey-fed pigs in southern areas or swill-fed pigs in the north-west. While control of the conditions is not complete, with cheap and highly nutritious feeding pigs will thrive. The whey and swill feeding is done in the yards and the copious and very liquid dung is squeegeed or hosed into a drain to run to a sludge tank, or else the outside yard may be slatted and the pigs lie in warm insulated kennels behind the yard. With solid-floored yards the cleaning can be carried out more easily and frequently by running a tractor straight through the yards with scraper blade attachments. This is effected by providing gates between the yards that swing back, enclosing the pigs in the pens and giving a clear run for the tractor.

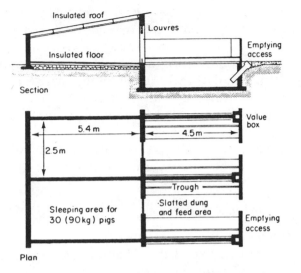

Fig. 12.9 Cottage-type piggery with open feeding/dunging area

Double-sided arrangements

An alternative approach with yarded piggeries is to have a covered yard allowing some build-up of muck, a central passage with troughs on each side, and kennels at the back for the pigs to lie in. The cleaning out is effected by swinging the gates back to the kennels and pushing through with tractor and blade attachment.

An original design of this form was produced by the late Mr. Stephen Horvat of Suffolk and various refinements which are now popular are referred to as Suffolk houses (Fig. 12.10); the centre area is uninsulated and naturally ventilated. The kennels at the back are well insulated and have flaps to control the air

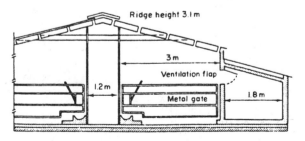

Fig. 12.10 Suffolk-type fattening house, with insulated kennels, covered yard and push-through mucking out

supply. Plenty of straw must be used in the yard and cleaning out should be frequent to maintain a healthy and dry atmosphere.

Several adaptations of the design have been produced, as the general arrangement of the 'Suffolk' house has a large following. It is a less expensive system than that of a totally enclosed piggery with troughs, probably varying from three-quarters to two-thirds of the cost.

Nowadays the 'Suffolk'-type of house is frequently built in the form of kennels under a covered yard (Fig. 12.11).

Monopitch fattening houses

Open-fronted units similar in concept to the 'Solari' farrowing house described earlier in this chapter are frequently used for fattening pigs. There are many minor variations but the

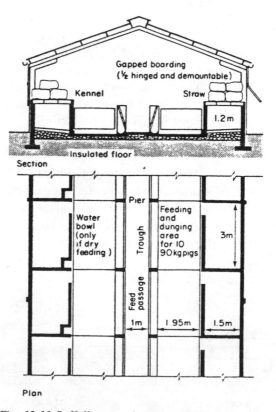

Fig. 12.11 Suffolk-type piggery in a covered yard

essentials are a simple design, space for up to 20 pigs in each pen, a warm lying area at the back, and exercise, feeding and dunging area at the front. All feeding systems can be used and dung cleaning operations vary from strawed floors and hand cleaning-out to slatted dunging areas and slurry disposal. If the general rules referred to are followed, the result can be very successful.

An absorbing study of the effect of different forms of fattening piggeries was carried out in Nebraska. This showed quite clearly that the open-fronted, monopitch fattening piggery gave the best all-round economic return compared with all other designs. The evidence is clear. Experiments over at least a quarter of a century in countries as climatically diverse as Sweden, Great Britain, Ireland, Canada, USA and South Africa show that simple designs that 'insulate and isolate' can give consistently good results.

Housing the sow

The strawed yard

A traditional, comfortable and healthy way of housing in-pig sows is to keep them in a completely covered yard. It keeps them well protected from bad weather, allows plenty of exercise and makes the provision of good stockmanship easy. Individual feeders can be provided and a suggested layout is shown in Fig. 12.12. The system is based on a line of feeders down one side of the yard which is raised above the general level of the yard itself – the higher the raised area the greater can be the build-up of muck before cleaning out is necessary. A drop of 750 mm will allow a build-up of approximately 3-4 months.

A suitable yard on these lines can be provided by having a span of 9 m and dividing it into bays of 4.5 m along its length. This gives a total area of about 40 m^2 per bay, which is suitable for ten sows. This is a convenient number, as the likelihood of fighting and bullying rises as the number kept together increases. Along one side the individual feeders have a length of 2.1 m including the trough, so that the actual lying and exercising area is just over 3.7 m^2 per sow.

Gates and fences between the sections of the yard should be easily removable to allow for cleaning. The construction of the

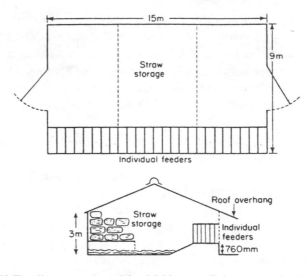

Fig. 12.12 Totally-covered yard for 25-30 sows. Ech sow needs about 3.7 m² of floor area, but it is best to keep the sows in small, evenly matched groups of about 10 sows

yard will be simple and uninsulated, but extra comfort can be provided by storing much of the straw on a platform above the strawed area, thus also making good use of the free space of the yard. Alternatively, the straw can be stored to one side of the yard under a lean-to extension. In both cases it can be thrown down on to the floor quite easily.

The ventilation of the yard is an important aspect that requires some careful attention. A yard of this type can be closed in on three sides – that is, the back and the two ends; the ridge must be left ventilated, either by using a capped open ridge or by installing chimney-type ventilating trunks. The front of the yard should face south and have an overhang of 1.5 m on the roof, which will give the pigman protection in feeding and also protect the yard from entry of snow or rain.

The base of the yard should be on concrete: this will not only assist in its cleaning, but also prevent the dangers of disease build-up which can always be a serious problem where ground is used continuously to keep livestock. The base of the walls of the yard can be of solid brick or concrete construction, and the remainder of the wall above this to the eaves of the yard can be in spaced boarding to give good ventilation.

Partly covered yard

A cheaper system and one which is probably little inferior in practice is to have only part of the yard strawed and covered and the remainder composed of a concreted yard for exercising and feeding, and containing individual feeders (Fig. 12.13). The simplest layout is similar to that in the totally covered yard, with the lying area at the back in the form of small kennels allowing 0.93 m^2 of lying area per sow, and a concreted area in front of 2.8 m^2 per sow. At the far side of the unit will be the individual feeders served by a concrete apron.

The sleeping area can be modestly constructed with an overall height of 1.5–1.8 m and will need insulation to prevent condensation and undue temperature fluctuations. To keep the sows dry and warm there should be a narrow step up into the pen and a small sill; the entrance need be only 750 mm wide and half-heck doors can be used for further ventilation, plus a sliding shutter at the back of the pen measuring 750 × 300 mm for a unit of eight sows.

Some breeders concerned with the number of foot and leg troubles that occur when sows are kept on built-up litter may

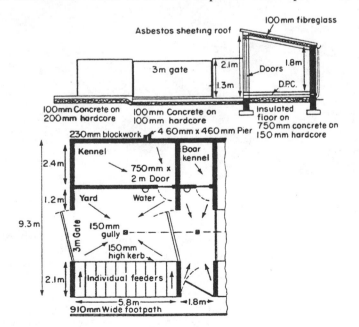

Fig. 12.13 Sow yard with individual feeders

Plate 7 Exterior view of sow yard with individual feeders

Plate 8 Interior view of sow yard

prefer this latter design, as the exercising on hard concrete may produce a healthier reaction on legs and feet.

Sow stalls

During pregnancy, sows tend to be aggressive to each other and when kept in groups the bullied animals may be injured or even killed, or their piglets may be stillborn, or they may abort. If there are no individual feeders, feeding may be very uneven, some sows receiving far too much and others becoming deficient. This is a very unsatisfactory state of affairs and so the *individual* housing of sows has a good deal to commend it to the farmer and the welfarist alike.

It may be of interest to note that it was something of an accident that sows were kept in this way because it was a chance trial by a Danish farmer which first produced the individual sow stall. Having given up keeping cows, he had a cowshed with standings available and as he was expanding in pigs he tried tethering in-pig sows in the same way. This system worked out well and the first sow stall was born, the sows being tethered through most of pregnancy on solid floored and bedded pens. From this developed the normal tethered system now prevalent and the sow stall in which the sow has no tether but has only freedom of movement to get up or lie down. Since the early days of the solid floored and bedded pens, developments have moved ahead to produce pens which have either partly or wholly slatted or perforated floors so there is automatic dung disposal, and bedding is rarely used.

The 'pros' and 'cons' of the system are evenly balanced. *For* the system is the absence of fighting, bullying and aggression of any sort; food and water are provided in adequate amount at all necessary times and the environment can be controlled to the finesse required; management is quite easy and inspection of the sows never a problem; sows in this system do tend to be docile and easy to handle.

Against the system are a substantial number of objections. The sows have no exercise for a long period; their boredom produces certain aberrant behaviours, such as the biting of bars in front of them and swaying from side to side; they have no contact with their mates, or almost none; sometimes, if the floor is badly finished, injuries occur to the feet and other parts; there may be sores around the tethers and elsewhere; there may be a higher incidence of prolapse; they usually have no bedding and no extra roughage can be consumed if needed by the sow; the sows need a higher temperature within their house as they have no way of keeping warm by close contact.

There are, however, a substantial number of alternative arrangements that can be used for the keeping of sows in pregnancy. It can be said of all of them that they do not entirely remove the risk of aggression by sow on sow and so they have to exist more competitively. However, ways of reducing this problem to a minimum are attempted. The arrangements have the advantage that sows are always in groups, which may be no more than 4 or 5 at the lower end of the scale; they will always have some bedding, and feeding is usually provided in individual stalls to ensure no bullying at this time.

Stall arrangements

A suitable design of tethered stall is shown in Fig. 12.14. The short tubular stall divisions are cheap and the open area at the back allows the sows considerable movement and makes cleaning out as easy as possible with a solid floor. Bedding may be used if desired. There is also a system of girth tethering which is preferred by some, since it allows a greater degree of movement.

There is an alternative arrangement with sows kept in confinement stalls without tethers. Tubular steel divisions are usual and may consist of horizontal rails only, or a combination of horizontal and vertical rails. Stall fronts are also normally railed and occasionally fitted with gates to allow easier movement of the sow. Rear gates may be solid, which is best when a partially slatted floor is used, to retain any surplus dung, or when bedding is used with a solid floor. The doors at the back may slide vertically or be hinged. With solid floor stalls vertically

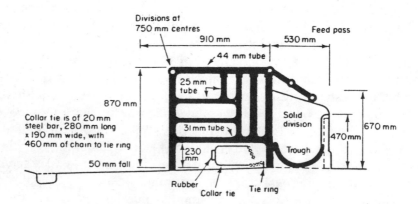

Fig. 12.14 Stall for tethered sow

sliding tubular gates or chains are used at the rear, the former being designed to clear the floor, so that cleaning out is facilitated. If a raised trough is used, the length of stalls is 1.95 m from the rear gate to the front edge of the trough, which forms an extra 375 mm, but if a sunken floor trough is used, a total length of 2.02 m is sufficient.

Plate 9 Tri-form concrete slats in sow stalls

Sow cubicles

Two interesting approaches have been evolved which keep sows in small groups. Sow cubicles consist of a group of three or four 2.1 m long × 600 mm wide free-choice cubicles for feeding and lying, with a communal dunging area behind them of 1.8 × 1.8 m. The unit would normally be placed under a covered yard with gates between dunging areas, which could be mechanically cleaned. Cubicles may also be placed in an outside hut with separate or communal dunging areas; one design has a door that can be opened and closed by the sow. These are most useful techniques to give a stress-free environment at minimum cost and with easy management.

Electronic sow feeding systems

Within the past two years a new arrangement has emerged for managing dry sows, based on the straw yard principle. This is a computer-controlled system providing automatic individual rationing of group-housed dry sows. It has been under extensive trial at the Ministry of Agriculture's Experimental Husbandry Farm at Terrington. As they have installed it, there is a central computer with keyboard and printer, controlling one or more feed stations. Each station can feed two separately housed groups of sows which obtain access in turn by swinging a hinged internal dividing gate in the feeder race. Every sow in the group wears a collar carrying an individually coded responder. When a sow enters the station an interrogator, located underneath the front of the trough, identifies her as the responder comes within range. If she has food due to her it is dispensed by an auger and rotating cup.

While feed is being dispensed, gates at the entrance to the station automatically lock shut behind the sow to prevent bullying and unless she chooses to leave the station they stay shut until she has eaten all her allocated ration. After the last feed drop she is allowed two minutes to eat any food which may have accumulated in the trough before the gates automatically unlock. Other animals attempting to enter the feed station then encourage her to back out so that her place can be taken by another sow. If a sow which has already had her full ration returns to the feed station, no further feed is dispensed, the back gates remain unlocked, and she has no incentive to stay there. The system has been fully described by Edwards (1985) who reports its successful use over a period of two years and with sows in groups of up to 34. By enabling accurate individual feeding to be carried out, it offers a real opportunity of reducing the cost yet improving the efficiency of the traditional straw yard housing system.

Housing the boar

Good housing is essential because it prolongs the boar's existence and use in the herd, and aids his fertility. Boars are very apt to 'go off their legs' and suffer from a number of mechanical troubles of the legs and limbs which may be less likely with good housing. Possibly the best way of keeping the boar is outside in a paddock, with a simple protection of a hut and a run. Where more confined accommodation is required, a simple system of sty and run is all that is needed, but the exercising area should be on generous lines. A covered area of around 3.7 m^2 and a yard of not less than 3.4 m^2 should be the aim. Part of the yarded area can form the service area or crate, which should be designed so that both the boar and the sow to be served can be easily moved around. This type of unit, as shown in Fig. 12.13, can be installed in the middle or at the end of a range of sow yards.

Another good way of keeping boars is to run them with a group of sows safely in-pig. No special accommodation is required in such cases – in fact a boar can be run with a group of up to eight sows under any of the other systems shown. Whatever system is used, it is generally an advantage to have the boar within sight, sound and smell of the weaned sows awaiting service, as there is evidence that this can have a beneficial effect in stimulating the onset of heat in the sow. He should also be able to see plenty of people and the general farm activity, which will tend to maintain his better temper and easier handling. It is certainly our experience that the most tractable boars are those who run with in-pig sows when not actually in use.

Accommodation for the newly weaned sow with boars

Because of the need to get sows served successfully as soon as possible after weaning, and since it is most likely to be achieved if they are kept close to the boar, it is preferable to give special consideration to this period. Most of the accommodation considered in this chapter incorporates boar units close to the sows or gilts, which will help to make the process of detecting heat and serving the females an easier and less laborious job. Farmers often prefer to place sows in this type of accommodation for about four weeks after weaning before they enter cubicles, stalls or tethers, or any other system, for the last three months of pregnancy.

Some points on capital costs and the 'alternative' systems

Carnell (Table 12.2) has estimated the capital costs of the different systems for keeping pigs. It can be seen that there is

Table 12.2 Some initial capital costs of pig production systems (adapted from Carnell, 1983)

	£/pig place
Dry sows	
Stalls, part slatted	325
Tethers, part slatted	305
Kennel and yard with individual feeders	410
Deep straw yard with individual feeders	470
Outdoor huts with fencing	60
Farrowing and lactation	
Farrowing house with crates, part slatted	870
Monopitch farrowing and rearing	750
Group suckling	500
Outdoor, insulated huts	320
Rearing	
Flat-deck cages	60
Verandahs	35
Weaner pool with straw	60
Monopitch	30

not a great deal of difference between the various indoor systems for housing breeders and dry sows, but the outdoor systems are markedly cheaper, as indeed are the simple rearing systems such as the monopitch as compared with the flat-deck cage. He also estimated that running costs of the indoor systems are not much less than outdoor – varying between as little as 1% more to a maximum of 11%. Hence it can be seen that the potential for profit is probably better for breeding pigs outside and using low-cost rearing methods. A strong word of caution is necessary to anyone contemplating outdoor pig keeping. It can only succeed where the following conditions apply:

1. Well drained and suitable land.
2. Good natural protection of the pigs by trees, hills, etc.
3. Appropriate breeds or strains of pigs.
4. Ideal equipment (not necessarily expensive!).
5. Dedicated management.
6. Full health control programmes.

References

Carnell, P. (1983) *Alternatives to Factory Farming*. London: Earth Resources Research Publication.

Edwards, S.A. (1985) 'Group housing systems for dry sows.' *Farm Building Progress* **80** 19–22.

13 Welfare and Cattle

Dairy Cows

The loose housing of dairy cows is now recognised as being the system most compatible with the welfare, comfort and cleanliness of the cows and can additionally be labour-saving. When planning the layout the following points must be considered:

1. Type of structure.
2. Method of feeding and storage of fodder.
3. Stock comfort and cleanliness.
4. Litter storage and use.
5. Drainage and disposal of dung and slurry.
6. Stock handling and isolation facilities.
7. Relationship to the milking parlour, cow circulation, and collecting and dispersal of cows from the parlour.

The distribution of types of housing is likely to be influenced by the probable rainfall of the area, which has a direct bearing on the amount of straw available at an economic price, the disposal of slurry and the size of the herd. As herd size increases there is a greater need for a system of loose housing and whatever the choice, the cleanliness of cows must play an important part if cows are to be milked quickly with proper attention given to hygiene.

For many years it was traditional to loose-house cattle in straw yards. In the main this was confined to fattening cattle and young stock, dairy cows being tied up in shippons or cowsheds. Beef cattle were more suited to yarding than a dairy herd as they tended to lie more quietly. Moreover, this was at a time when most dairy cows had horns, so grouping together in yards could lead to bullying and injuries. However, when dairy cows were dehorned, housing cows in straw yards increased. Initially, certain fundamental errors were made, e.g. cows being fed on

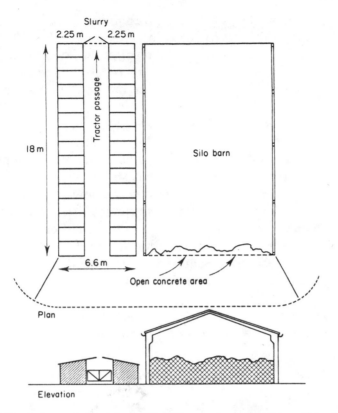

Slurry

2.25 m   2.25 m

Tractor passage

18 m

Silo barn

6.6 m

Open concrete area

Plan

Elevation

Fig. 13.1 Typical cow-kennel layout for 30 cows incorporating self-feed silage

the bedded area adding to the straw requirement, lack of knowledge of optimum space requirements, and so on.

The housing area can be fully or partly covered (Fig. 13.1) and may include a separate feeding area, which may be in the open or under cover. A covered area for the storage of fodder and straw may also be required as a part of the layout.

Many units have been built up around a central silo barn with lean-tos up to 9 m wide on one or both sides (a width of 9 m is unsuitable for conversion to cubicles). Siting for possible extension is important and so is the provision of adequate headroom for mechanical cleaning-out. Allowance must also be made for a build-up of dung to a depth of 1 m or more, which may require alterations to the height of gates.

In-filling is usually in brick or blockwork between the stanchions to a height of 2–2.5 m with, where necessary, some form of cladding above this. An extension to the eaves on a cantilever or bracket giving an overhang of about 1 m protects the bedded area from driving rain. The importance of adequate ventilation to reduce the risk of respiratory conditions in dairy cows and young stock is now fully recognised. The use of space boarding above the blockwork is one method of obtaining a free flow of air (see Chapter 7).

Disappointing results have frequently been experienced with cows housed in straw yards, and correct management is essential for success. The bedded area should be used solely as a place for cows to lie down and entry onto this should be along the length of one side and not through a narrow opening. This will prevent unnecessary trampling on straw and reduce litter usage. Feeding arrangements and water troughs should be sited on an unbedded concrete area which is also required for exercise.

The amount of space required for the bedded area is 3.7 m^2 per cow, and at least 1.8 m^2 per cow of concrete exercise and feed area. Trough space required per cow is 600 mm. With a properly managed yard, straw usage is likely to be about 500–600 kg per cow per winter of 150 days.

The cubicle

A completely different approach to housing dairy cows was pioneered in the early 1960s by Howell Evans. This combined features of both cowshed housing and yarding systems and, with modifications, has become known as cubicle and cow kennel housing. Cubicles are single stalls with a partition between each cow, constructed within a building and having a passage-way of concrete or slatted floor construction, allowing access to the cubicles and also forming an area where slurry dung can be collected and cleaned away. Cows are not tied and are free to exercise, drink or feed at will. Feeding and watering facilities are provided in a separate area from the cubicle or lying area.

Kennels are an extension of the cubicle system, each kennel being a cubicle complete with its own wall and roof. They are usually constructed in batches with end walls, so forming a building on their own. Construction can be in timber or metal.

The first cubicle sheds were designed for comparatively small numbers of dairy cows. As herd and shed sites increased, various problems of management became apparent; these included refusals, injuries, lameness and mastitic infections of types hitherto rarely encountered. Subsequent developments have introduced measures which aim to combat these problems.

This type of housing now has several advantages which include:

1. Most cows keep cleaner than in other systems of loose housing.
2. There is economy of bedding material, generally at a lower cost than strawed yards.
3. The bedded area can be constructed within a relatively cheap structure.
4. With proper planning the system can be completely flexible, including feeding arrangements and the possibility of extension.

In any system of cubicle housing the basic requirements in its design and construction are:

Construction of the floor – size and material for the bed.
Type of cubicle divisions and head rails.
Adequate ventilation to provide the correct environment.
Disposal of slurry.
Ease of day-to-day management.

Construction of the floor and bed

The size of the cubicle is important, for dimensions which were adequate when they were first introduced may no longer be large enough for herds in which, for example, Holstein blood has been introduced. To err on the generous side with dimensions is less likely to lead to difficulties with refusals. As the number of cows in a unit has increased, there has been a tendency, on the grounds of cost, to allow too little space for cows to move around comfortably. Therefore the first rule is that the building shall be of adequate size to allow sufficient room for cows to behave as individuals and with cubicle beds large enough to enable the largest cow to lie down, rest and rise in complete comfort. Badly designed buildings are likely to create hazards and stress to cows and operators alike and thereby predispose stock to health problems. This may be seen where buildings have been adapted without sufficient thought being given to the best environmental conditions.

Suggested sizes for each cubicle are:

Average cow weight (kg)	Length (mm)	Width (mm)
Over 650	2 240	1 200
400–650	2 120	1 100
Under 400	2 000	1 000

It is usual for the passageway, which may service one or two rows of cubicles, to have a width of 2 100 mm. When planning the layout no places should be left where dominant cows can prevent others from reaching vacant cubicle beds, the silage face, mangers or out-of-parlour feeders. All concrete areas should have a non-slip finish.

The original cubicle bed had a concrete or wooden heelstone some 150–225 mm high. The bed was then filled with a variety of materials, some of which were often available locally, e.g. sand, sawdust and chalk. These met with varying degrees of success. Disadvantages could be their high cost, lack of availability and that some required too much maintenance. With some there was evidence that they were connected with mastitic problems.

Whatever material is used, the floor profile should be sloping slightly from front to back and be firm, safe, comfortable and dry. The type of base chosen will be permanent, e.g. concrete or bitumen macadam, or of materials such as chalk or earth which may require frequent or annual maintenance.

Concrete. This provides a permanent and relatively maintenance-free bed, usually formed from 100 mm of plain dense concrete over a hardcore base blinded with sand. Before laying the concrete it is advisable to lay a heavy duty PVC damp-proof membrane on top of the sand.

Opinions vary over the desirability of constructing a lip to the cubicle bed. Advantages of having a lip are that it helps to retain the litter and less will be pushed off the bed. But they are more difficult to clean and may allow dirty, wet bedding material to build up, which is undesirable. If an insulated cubicle bed is used without litter there should be no lip. Those without a lip should be given a wood float finish which will help to retain the bedding. Lipped cubicles should have a smooth finish.

Bitumen Macadam. The cubicle is constructed as usual with a concrete heelstone 150–225 mm wide, with a well rammed hardcore base. A layer of 'dense' bitumen Macadam is laid over the base to a depth of 75 mm, with a fall of approximately 75 mm from head to heelstone. To allow for shrinkage the macadam should be slightly proud of the heelstone and the cubicle should not have a lip. For successful results it is essential to use the 'dense' type of material and to ensure that it is thoroughly compacted.

Other materials can be successfully used, but this is less common than hitherto. They are: dry, stone-free soil, rammed chalk or sand. Regular maintenance is essential. The type of sand used is most important; it should be non-abrasive, free from large particles, non-staining and not of a muddy texture. Mushroom chalk free from flints and well compacted with a vibrating roller is also satisfactory.

It is usual to cover most beds with litter to provide warmth and comfort. Requirements for litter are that it should be non-toxic and easily degradable, absorbent, and cause no skin damage. Choice will be guided by price, availability and method of slurry disposal. Materials used are long or chopped straw, sawdust or shavings, shredded newsprint and sand.

The use of chopped straw offers several advantages. Less material is used, there is a considerable saving in time and labour, and the bed is drier and the cows cleaner.

Where sawdust or wood shavings are used it should preferably be from softwood, free from hard splinters and not have been treated with any toxic materials. It is absorbent and easy to handle but its use has been associated with coliform mastitis.

Mats and carpeting are also sometimes used on a concrete base and are claimed to improve cow comfort and reduce the litter requirement. Materials used for this purpose are rubber, polyester, or PVC. Thickness varies and it can be laid as individual mats secured with studs or in carpet rolls. One type consists of three layers of different materials. Tiles made of thermoplastic bitumen can be laid on existing concrete beds and have given satisfactory results.

The kerb or step at the back of the cubicle is to prevent slurry being pushed on to the bed when the passageways are scraped, and it can also help to retain litter on the bed. These are usually rectangular blocks of treated timber or concrete about 75 mm in width and 200–250 mm high. The width of the passageway will usually be approximately 2 100 mm but where a feed fence or manger is an integral part of the cubicle shed the concrete passage between the manger and heelstone should be 3 000 to 3 500 mm wide.

Cubicle divisions, head-rails and brisket boards

Much of the success of cubicle housing will depend on the design of the cubicle divisions and their correct installation. Difficulties which can occur range from refusals to behavioural problems and physical damage to the legs and teats.

Since the introduction of this type of housing, many different designs of division have been tried. They have been constructed of tubular or box-profile steel or wood. Sufficient room and correct dimensions are likely to be most important, but there are many situations where different types of division have been used successfully.

Figures 13.2 and 13.3 show several types of division bases and typical dimensions. These should be such that cows can rise and lie down without restriction and with safety, and lie in comfort.

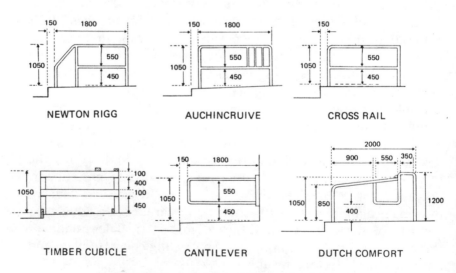

Fig. 13.2 Some cubicle divisions for dairy cows

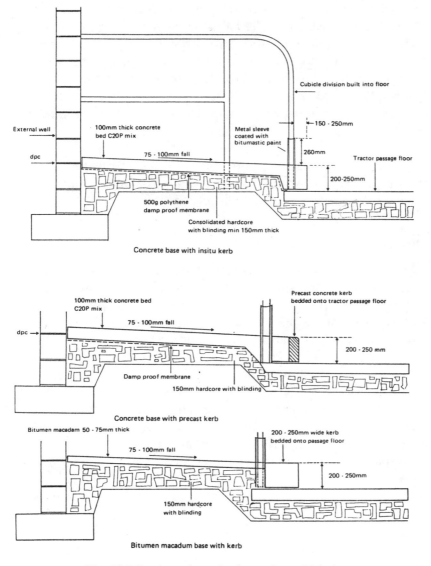

Fig. 13.3 Sections through alternative cubicle bases

To avoid the risk of cows getting trapped, the height of the lower rail of the division to the finished level of the bed should be between 400–450 mm. If the rail is too low there is a risk of a cow trapping and possibly breaking a leg. A flexible lower 'rail' can be made from a polypropylene rope suitably tensioned. The recommended distance from the bed to the lower rail of the Dutch comfort cubicle division is 400 mm.

As with the cowshed, the aim with cubicles is for the cow to stand in the bed so that any dung falls into the passageway. To help to position the cow correctly it may be beneficial to fix a head-rail or brisket board which will prevent her standing too far forward. The head-rail may be fixed some 450–550 mm from the front of the cubicle although it is essential to choose the exact distance in relation to the height of the rail. The brisket board should be placed at the same distance from the front of the cubicle as the head-rail and the kerb should be no higher than 100 mm, to avoid injuries.

Disposal of slurry and drainage

In traditional semi-solid systems of housing this presented few problems but with cubicle systems and a greater awareness of the dangers of pollution of watercourses, the disposal of slurry and liquid effluent has come to require great care. Cubicle passageways and concrete feed and other areas should be scraped at least once a day and preferably twice. The problem of collection, storage and disposal of dung and slurry can be solved in many cases by using capital equipment which may be expensive to install and operate and which may ultimately influence the system of farming policy. Whatever system of disposal is adopted, it is essential firstly to consider the requirements of legislation, both of public and of animal health; there are also social considerations which may be the subject of legislation for both safety and the risk of causing a 'nuisance'. Proximity to villages, dwellings, and watercourses must decide the practicability of methods of waste disposal, and each case must be designed for a particular set of circumstances.

Day-to-day management

There are several points in the day-to-day management of the cubicles which should help to keep the bed clean, dry and safe. Daily maintenance should include:

1. Removal of dung pats from the bed.
2. Twice-a-day scraping of the passageways, which should help to avoid slurry being carried onto the bed.

3. Littering the bed as required. Frequency will depend on the type of litter. Fresh litter should be delivered to the front of the cubicle bed. Where chopped straw or newsprint is used a dry, compacted layer will help to retain the fresh litter when added.

After cows have been milked they usually like to return to the cubicle to lie down, so where possible, these jobs should be carried out either before or whilst the cows are being milked. As the udder is especially vulnerable to infection just after milking, a clean, dry bed will reduce this risk.

The success or failure of any cubicle housing will depend to a large extent on the way in which the cows have been conditioned. Where cows are nervous and stressed the best design may fail, resulting in injuries and behavioural problems. Where they are contented they are much more likely to adapt to any system, even when the layout or construction is less than ideal.

Problems which can occur in the design of cubicle beds, and their possible effect, are as tabulated:

Cubicle design	Possible results
Too long and/or too wide.	Allows too much freedom of movement with soiling of beds and dirty cows.
Too short and/or too narrow.	Makes rising difficult which causes bruising to the hocks, pelvis and shoulders. These injuries can cause high refusal rates or cows lying back over the kerb. Where the cubicle is too short the cows tend to rise front first as there is insufficient room to move forward.
Bottom rail too low.	Possible injury to pelvis, shoulder and ribs and risk of leg injuries.
Bottom rail too high.	Injury to pelvis through rising front first.
Head rail too far from the front.	Injury to knees and teats. Lying back over the kerb and difficulty in rising.

Low head rail.	Injury to knees and neck and cut teats.
Kerb too high.	Bruised heels and high refusal rate.
Badly maintained beds with broken concrete and pro-truding stones.	Injuries to knees and hocks. Cut teats and general stress.
Slippery base.	Injuries to shoulder and pin-bones and difficulty in rising.
Rough and new concrete.	Damage to hooves, knees and hocks.

Facilities for handling cattle

With the general increase in herd size there is more need to provide facilities for the segregation and treatment of dairy cows. A well-planned system should mean a saving of time for the stockman and veterinary surgeon as well as being safer for both operators and stock and causing less stress.

The basic units which have to be considered are: a diversion box to separate individual cows on leaving the parlour; a race and crush for the treatment of animals on a herd basis and to provide isolation; and calving boxes.

The diversion box for separating out one cow at a time is best arranged at the parlour exit after the cow has been milked. This can be achieved by using a shedding gate or door which can be operated from the parlour pit or work area by remote control. It is an advantage to have individual stalls in the diversion area for veterinary treatment or artificial insemination.

The cattle handling unit

The requirements for this are gathering pens, a forcing funnel and a race and crush. It is an advantage to have a shedding gate after the crush.

The layout should be situated as close as possible to the parlour. Often, concrete collecting yards can be used as the gathering pen, which will reduce costs and areas of concrete to be cleaned and will also fit in with the cows' normal behaviour pattern.

General requirements are:

1. Access to the head and rear of the animal.
2. Animals securely restrained for the safety of stock and operators.
3. Crush preferably under cover.
4. All services available, i.e. electric light and power and hot and cold water.

For the gathering pen about 1.4–1.85 m^2 per cow should be allowed. The forcing funnel can have one side in line with the race and the other side at an angle of 20–30° to guide the cows into the race. A splay on one side only will guide one cow at a time into the race, whereas a double splay may allow two together to try to enter.

Ideally the handling race should be designed to hold up to four adult cattle, which will require a length of just over 9 m and a width of 675–700 mm. Construction can be with tubular metal or sawn timber uprights and rails, or a combination of both. The height of the race should be approximately 1 500 m, with the bottom rail 250 mm from the ground and three more rails to make up the required height. Access to animals along both sides is desirable.

The requirements for a suitable 'crush' are:

1. The animal must be securely restrained.
2. The head, neck, feet, udder, flanks and rear of the animal should be accessible for inspection and treatment.
3. The crush should be adjustable to take all types of cattle.
4. The design and construction should not be such as to cause injury to cattle or handlers.
5. It should be relatively quiet and firmly secured.
6. It should have a free-standing roof if it is outside a building.

Many tubular steel crushes with removable panels are available and it may be possible to incorporate them into the handling system so that the crush can be portable and used for outlying young stock when required. At the end of the crush a shedding gate is desirable to sort out cattle for further treatment or dispersal.

A cattle-handling layout (Fig. 13.4) has been designed by the West of Scotland Agricultural College, which incorporates most of the features referred to above to ensure the steady movement of cattle in safety for both cattle and operator, and to enable the

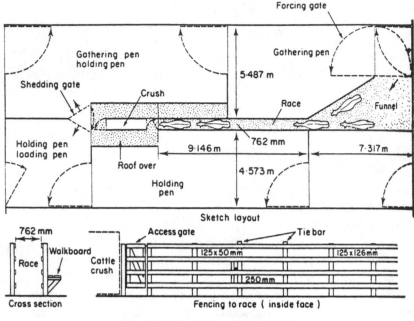

Fig. 13.4 Cattle-handling facilities

whole area to be kept clean, having services available for washing down and a supply of electricity for a hand inspection lamp, clippers, hot water and de-horning.

Calving boxes and isolation facilities

Cattle may need to be isolated for various reasons, e.g. because of injury, or when calving, or to prevent the spread of disease. It is essential that cattle really can be kept isolated and that healthy animals are kept away; that drainage, straw and dung can be disposed of separately and without causing any danger of infection to other stock; and that the boxes can be effectively cleaned and disinfected as required. A suggested size for an isolation box is 4 200 × 3 600 and 2 600 mm high; there should be one box for every 25 cows in the herd. A suitable construction is shown in Fig. 13.5.

Plenty of light and ventilation will be required, and as the box may be housing sick animals, insulation of the roof and floor will help to keep the box more comfortable. Division walls should be taken to full height.

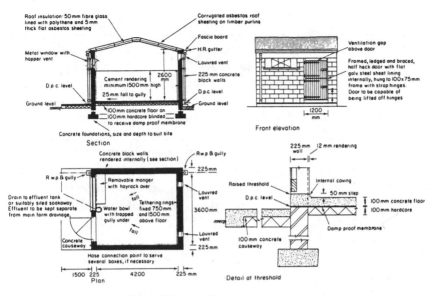

Fig. 13.5 Isolation box for cattle

It is important to include some method of securing cattle, either by ties, a head yoke or a holding gate. A nose-ring may also be an advantage for restraining animals which are difficult to handle. Facilities for milking cows need to be available, and where the boxes are some distance from the milking parlour, a separate vacuum pump could be necessary and provision made for disposal of milk.

As it may be necessary to move a carcase from the box, or as an animal may lie across a door and be unable to rise, special attention should be given to this aspect. Doors should be at least 1 200 mm wide and be hung to open outwards and such that the doors can be lifted off their hinges. A half-heck stable-type door is recommended so that animals can be observed without the stockman having to enter the box.

The requirements for calving boxes are similar, although there is not likely to be the same need for segregation, and the number required in a herd will depend upon the calving pattern and the management of cows after calving. One box for every 20 cows in the herd is suggested where the calvings are evenly spaced throughout the year.

Foot-care

Care of feet in dairy cows is essential to avoid falling milk yields and severe culling. Most lameness starts in the feet, and the causes may be interlinked. While husbandry factors are important, the shape and soundness of feet are inherited characters, so it is important to breed from bulls whose progeny have feet which are without defects and are sound and long-lasting. The quality of the horn of the foot can be influenced by the quantity and composition of the feed. High-protein feed increases growth rate and tends to produce softer horn, and deficiencies of vitamin A will also cause deterioration in horn quality. Also, standing in pools of slurry for long periods, or travelling a lot in muddy lanes or standing in badly poached kale fields are all predisposing causes of softness of the feet and susceptibility to injuries. Feet which are soft allow small stones or other sharp objects to break the skin and produce a suitable condition for invasion by bacteria which may cause foul-in-the-foot. The texture of concrete floors can also cause soreness in the feet, and this appears to be particularly so when the floor is laid with a rough surface and when the concrete is 'green'. In most cases the soreness disappears as the concrete 'cures' and there is some surface wear.

In order to reduce some of those conditions which lead to softness of the feet and thereby lessen the risk of infection, the construction of tracks for the movement of cows from the parlour to the grazing area has been tried on many farms. There are also other advantages apart from the one to cows' feet, these being the quicker movement of cows, cleaner cows and less poaching of grassland. The tracks can also be used during silage making and for transporting slurry in winter. The tracks can be constructed from various materials, some of which could be available locally. The base will usually be hardcore, and this can be topped off or blinded with chalk, quarry dust or other materials which do not contain large or sharp particles. A more permanent but more costly surface could be a 75–150 mm concrete roadway. A suitable width is 3–4.5 m, although it is possible for wider tracks to have a range of uses.

The regular use of a foot-bath will help to harden the horn of the hoof as well as acting as a preventative against infection. The foot-bath can be constructed in either single or double sections. Where there are two sections, the first will contain clean water to act as a foot-wash prior to treatment. Foot-baths are usually sited at the parlour exit but can in practice be situated in any position where cows must pass through them. Suitable dimensions are: width 900–1 050 mm, length 2 100–2 400 mm and depth a minimum of 75 mm. The bottom of the bath should be shaped in corrugated ridges running the length of the bath to splay the claws of the hoof. The width from the top of one corrugation to the next should be 50–60 mm. Non-slip entry to and exit from the bath are important. It should be possible to drain the solution from the bath quickly so that it can be scrubbed out and flushed. Drainage should only be allowed to discharge at a point where it cannot pollute any watercourse. A 3% copper sulphate or 10% formalin solution is usually used, and it is important that the bath be kept clean.

The bull pen

An essential adjunct for the dairy farm is safe, strong and comfortable accommodation for the bull. Figure 13.6 shows a double pen designed by the West of Scotland Agricultural College which incorporates the following essential features:

1. Adequate covered space and a good exercising area, providing completely healthy environment.
2. Sliding doorways between the box and yard which can be remotely controlled from pulley ropes outside. There are also sliding doorways into the feeding passage, which enables complete security to be maintained.
3. A feeding passage conveniently placed so both pens can be serviced in safety and under cover.
4. The exercising yards incorporate service pens and there are two steel stanchions screening off a small corner of the yard as a refuge in the event of emergency while the yard is being cleaned out. The service pens are safety devices consisting of a short passage approximately 1 m wide internally and separated from the yard, except during service, by a 'control' gate approximately 2.1 m long and 2 m high. This gate is hinged in such a way that the cow may be admitted to the service pen from outside the buildings while the bull is confined to the yard.

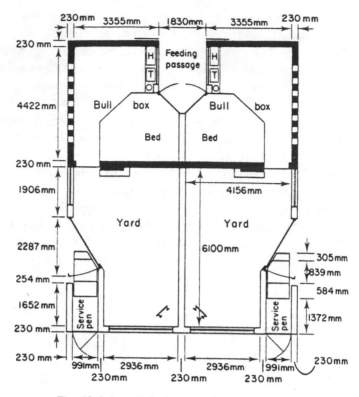

Fig. 13.6 A well-designed pair of bull boxes

5. The design shown here should be strongly built; solid double brickwork is recommended. It should be rendered on the inside. A tethering system by overhead cable is often utilised. This consists of a strong steel cable stretched diagonally from a point about 1.7 m above floor level at the feed trough across the pen and exercising yard to a point about 1.9 m above ground level at the far corner of the service pen. The bull is tethered to this cable by a chain fastened at one end with a slip-hook to his nose-ring and to the cable at the other end by a free-sliding runner-ring. In order that the weight of the tether chain is not taken on the nose-ring, the slip-hook is also attached to a short chain harness led round the horns and down through the ring. The tether-chain is long enough to allow the bull to lie down and use the service pen but is short enough to prevent him reaching at least two corners of his box and yard, respectively.

Calf housing

Traditionally, calves would either be born in the open, where rough shelter would be provided, or they would be placed in the corner of the cowshed or in a loose box. Under these circumstances the challenge of disease was normally very low or non-existent and calves were well able to withstand the normal fluctuations in temperature – so long as the protected place was dry and draught-free. However, when cattle herds became larger and the rearing of calves developed into larger units, the placing of considerable numbers of calves in one building led to much greater difficulties with disease control and the weakened calves seemed to need much better environmental control. This led to a mistaken policy of giving the calves accommodation in fully controlled environment housing, and developing large buildings with many calves in them, run on a continuous basis, and with environmental control in the hands of the fan and the thermostat. Not surprisingly, on consideration of points made earlier in the book, such systems were often capable of causing great trouble with the environment. Artificial heating was rarely used except in veal calf houses, and either modest amounts of bedding were used or none at all.

Calves in many systems were housed in individual and small pens so that they had no personal choice as to where they lay. The great difficulty was to get the right balance between good ventilation, draughts, damp and warmth, and in many cases the housing totally failed to achieve this. The result was a combination of poor productivity and high disease incidence, especially of respiratory diseases. Even attempts at greatly increasing the thermal insulation of the building and reducing the air space to a much lower capacity would usually not work.

Now, after considerable experimentation and development, and a return to fundamentals the following is clear:

1. Young calves, like all young stock, should be kept to a minimum disease challenge in very early life. This means in effect that the housing should not put many calves together and each part of the unit should be run on an all-in, all-out basis.
2. High temperatures are not required at all, so long as air movement is low and the calf is dry and well bedded.

3. Low air movement, and probably also low ventilation rates, cannot be easily arranged in totally enclosed buildings. Therefore the most satisfactory solution is the monopitch house, general details of which are given in Fig. 13.7. Here, copious space is ensured, and a measure of choice left to the calf according to the weather conditions, so it may go to the rear of the building in the cold weather and come forward in the hot.

4. The major importance of dividing the building up into completely separate 'cells' cannot be emphasised enough and it is best to have no more than 5–10 calves in one air space.

There are certain other details that should be very carefully attended to. The major diseases affecting calves are respiratory and enteric. The former is primarily dealt with by the overall measure we have already given. So far as curbing enteric disease is concerned, a division into small units is a major factor. So also are drainage and bedding, and a very good way of achieving this is to have a good slope on the floor to a gully in front and place over this wooden slats and then the bedding. The slats will help the seepage and reduce the bedding required: otherwise it is quite satisfactory without the slats, but in that case more bedding will be required.

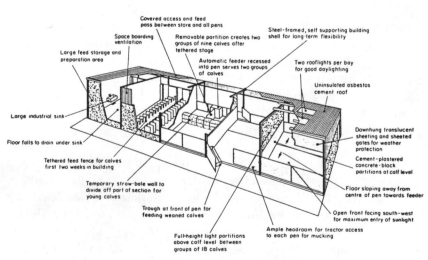

Fig. 13.7 Monopitch calf house

Beef cattle

Until recently beef cattle, when housed, were kept on very traditional lines, in strawed yards in buildings constructed in locally available materials – brick, stone or timber. Sometimes beef calves are single- or multiple-suckled on nurse cows for periods up to six months. In cases like this the cows are tied up on standings on one side of a building, which also contains the calf pens along the opposite side across a wide service passageway to allow vehicles to come into the building and assist with cleaning.

A few beef cattle are still tied up for fattening, though this is now rare, so that nearly all beef cattle are now yarded. Details of the construction for good welfare are similar to those for dairy cows. The amount of straw required for litter is usually high; yards may be fully covered, or part-covered, with an open area for feeding. In the latter case it is usual to concrete the open area and arrange cribs and racks along the outside to facilitate feeding. The advantage of this system is that a smaller covered area is required and less straw needed.

Table 13.1 Recommendations for slatted floor beef units

	Area/ beast (m^2)	Slat size (mm)	Gap between slats (mm)	Trough space/ beast (mm)
Calves up to 4 months	1.1	50–38	32	380
Yearlings	1.4–1.8	100–75	38	380–510
Beef steers and heifers (over 500 kg)	1.8–2.3	130–100	38	600
Cows	3.2–3.7	130–100	38	600–750

A substantial number of beef cattle are housed on slats in covered yards and the recommendations given in Table 13.1 are made to give as good conditions as possible, although it is again emphasised that cattle will do better, and their welfare will be safeguarded better, on bedded floors.

A cautionary word is necessary on the fattening of bulls for beef. They should be kept in groups of no more than 8–10, and once the group is established it should not change. Pen divisions must be strong and at least 1.5 m high. Walls must be very strong too, gates and doors child-proof and some refuge areas should be provided in the pens, with feeding and bedding servicing carried out from outside.

14 Welfare and Poultry

Over the past 70 years or so systems of poultry management have developed and changed at an incredible speed. At the beginning of the period birds were either scavengers around the farmyard or were kept in small permanent huts and runs – a semi-intensive system. It was often a problem for them to survive and it is well known that birds kept in these ways consumed a great deal of food and produced far fewer eggs than they were genetically capable of doing, whilst many of the eggs were either lost or were 'stale' by the time they were collected. Certain diseases were of high incidence and foxes and other predators could be highly destructive. In really bad weather egg-laying would be greatly reduced or could stop altogether. Obviously there was little future for this system as even the traditional farmyard for the birds to roam over has now disappeared.

Side by side with this there were some free-range birds kept on fields, and then followed the first of the forerunners to the modern, intensive arrangements. 'Domestic poultry keepers' kept their birds in small houses and open runs, an arrangement more or less the same as the semi-intensive system. Whilst the birds kept in this way were allowed plenty of movement, they could also suffer terribly from the weather and a build-up of infection and there was also an opportunity of vices developing. Labour, maintenance and housing costs were all high and the system ended up by being neither viable economically nor desirable from the welfare angle.

A better system, developed in the 1930s, was the 'fold unit', with birds kept in small groups with a hut and run that were moved regularly across pasture so that the birds were kept in a healthy and stimulating environment. Unfortunately the system was too expensive for the production of commercial eggs but, with adaptation, remains as an excellent method for the rearing of game birds. Also about this time came the first fully intensive system with birds housed all the time in quite large groups of several hundred with plenty of windows giving good natural lighting, perches and droppings boards, and straw litter which was frequently cleaned out. This was potentially a useful arrangement but, unfortunately, knowledge on the nutritional requirements of birds and the control of disease were insufficient to sustain this system and so it largely died out.

It was also at about this same period that the first of the battery systems appeared, but at this time they were quite spacious cages and had only one bird housed to a cage. They were, however, an expensive method of housing and did not have a substantial following.

In the 1940s and '50s came a veritable explosion of new techniques, some good and some bad. Most are still with us today, modified in one form or another. During this period the birds' nutritional needs were largely satisfactorily elucidated, disease control methods improved dramatically, and the importance of environmental control, including the complete regulation of lighting, were fully appreciated.

The henyard with a large, strawed open yard in front of a covered 'lean-to' was used with some success but had difficulties with rain, snow, parasites and vermin; the deep-litter system was born again – actually after a lapse of about a century – and remains as a principal system for breeders, broilers and a few commercial egg-layers. The totally slatted floor house had a brief spell of popularity in the 1960s but proved to be one of the most difficult to manage and tended to produce flighty, temperamental birds, prone to every known vice in their communal boredom. Whilst it has disappeared in the UK, it is still seen overseas, especially in the USA, and with the right type of bird can be rather more successful.

Soon after the slatted floor house appeared it was found, by accident rather than design, that if two birds were placed together in a single birdcage, each bird actually laid more eggs than if placed separately. The implications of this were enormous – housing and capital costs could be reduced to less than half overnight. Thereafter many investigations were made by farmers and others to find the optimum, and the end result was that it was established that the best commercial results were achieved by placing 3 to 5 birds in a cage within an area that is about a third of that which used to be allowed to a single bird in a cage. From this stage, further development stacked the birds higher and in a more compressed fashion so that the battery cage as we now know it emerged. With the automation of feeding, watering and egg collection, no other system could compete economically, such were its advantages. Various cage systems are shown in Fig. 14.1.

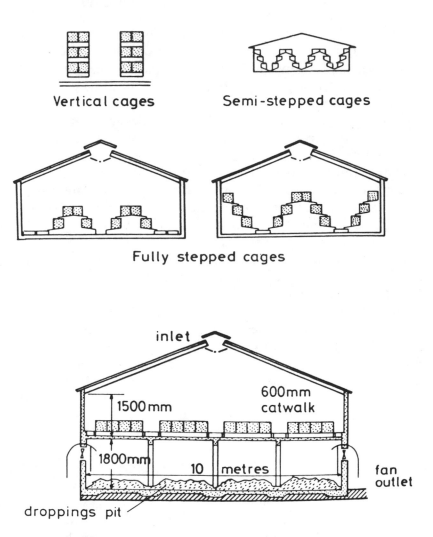

Fig. 14.1 Cage systems

The multi-bird battery cage is an extraordinarily efficient method of keeping laying birds and it is difficult for alternative methods to match its cost advantages. Birds are housed more tightly than in any other system – about 450 cm^2 being a reasonably generous allowance by modern standards. Cages are stacked 3, 4 or even up to 6 cages high. With such a high density it is comparatively cheap and easy to give the birds the degree of warmth, ventilation, air movement and lighting required in well insulated, windowless, mechanically ventilated houses. Eggs are clean, and feeding, watering and egg collection can all be done automatically. Health is usually good, or at least disease and mortalities are low since the wire floor separates birds from their droppings; it also separates groups of 3 to 5 in their cages from other birds and maintains a uniform distribution of birds within the house. Vices are controlled by judicious regulation of lighting and/or trimming of the upper beak to make feather-pulling difficult.

These are all powerful economic facts. Against these we set the welfare argument. The birds have very limited movement. They can barely preen, can stretch their limbs only to a small extent and can only just turn round. They do have easy access to water and food. They are denied litter and dust-baths, the method by which a bird cleans itself. There is no real exercise in the cage. Birds in cages tend to lose feathering, especially around the neck and breast, so higher temperatures need to be maintained in the house in order to ensure warmth for the poorly covered bird. There are also some doubts about the ability of the stockman to care for birds properly, as it may be difficult to inspect the birds effectively, especially in the lower and topmost cages. There are grave dangers that if something vital goes wrong, such as a power failure or interruption of the water or food supply, a disaster can take place and even, as has happened in some cases, all the birds perish.

There has been some interest in the 'Get-away' cage (Fig. 14.2) which provides birds in cages with more space, a perch, and littered nest box. Regrettably, after some ten years' experience it has not been found commercially viable.

However, other, more successful 'alternatives' to the battery are beginning to flourish, not least because eggs from birds kept under these systems may command considerably higher prices in the shops.

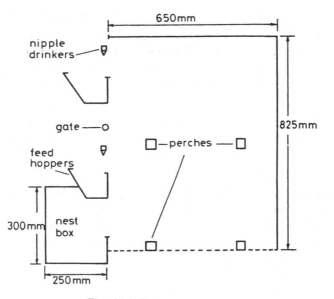

Fig. 14.2 Get-away cage

The main systems which qualify for the description of 'alternatives' are:

1. Modified free-range.
2. Covered straw yard.
3. Aviary with deep litter.

It will be realised that the cost of producing laying eggs under any of these alternative systems will be greater than the cost of eggs produced from birds in cages.

The extra costs will be divided in a variable way between all the factors, from greatly increased capital costs of some of the alternative systems used, to extra costs on labour and feed, and additional losses from mortality and broken or second quality eggs. It may be emphasised that these extra costs can be subject to considerable modification by skilful use of resources and by ingenuity in the maintenance of the environment and use of labour. The extra costs are also mainly incurred in temperate climates such as the British Isles or Northern Europe. In warmer countries the extra running costs may well be substantially reduced. It is encouraging to find that the costs are by no means prohibitive and if the public is prepared to pay a modest extra amount they can have their eggs produced in systems where birds have a more generally acceptable housing and environment.

Some helpful figures are available to give a good measure of accuracy as to how much the extra costs of alternative systems really are. Table 14.1 shows that no systems can compete with the cage in its low capital cost, the outlay for the other systems varying between about 20 and 60% more. Calculated perform-ance data in Table 14.2 also gives a clear advantage to the cage but extra costs at the worst extreme, comparing free-range with battery birds, indicate costs up by only about 20%. These figures were gleaned from many sources and represent an amalgam of evidence. However, in a recent trial at the Ministry of Agriculture's Husbandry Farm (Table 14.3), birds in straw yards performed better than anticipated and indeed laid as many eggs as a caged bird, although costs would remain higher on capital, food and labour.

Table 14.1   Capital costs per bird (from Carnell, 1983)

System	Total costs (building and eqiupment) £
Cages	5.50
Deep litter (1.5 ft²/bird)	7.50
Aviary (0.5 ft²/bird)	7.30
Straw yard	7.50
Semi-intensive	8.50
Free-range	8.00

This shows that whilst no 'alternative' system can compete in *capital* cost to that of the cage system, it is possible to create viable alternatives which need not be prohibitively costly.

The covered straw yard

The basis of the covered straw yard is a simple shed, uninsulated and naturally ventilated, but giving good protection from the weather. An ideal structure is either an open-fronted monopitch (lean-to) or simple pitched roof building, as shown in Fig. 14.3. The building will be about 6 m deep or across, with the open

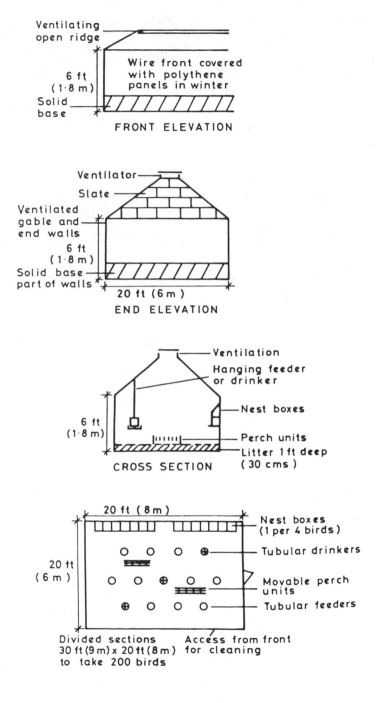

Ventilating open ridge

Wire front covered with polythene panels in winter

6 ft (1·8 m)

Solid base

FRONT ELEVATION

Ventilator

Slate

Ventilated gable and end walls

6 ft (1·8 m)

Solid base part of walls

20 ft (6 m)

END ELEVATION

Ventilation

Hanging feeder or drinker

6 ft (1·8 m)

Nest boxes

Perch units

Litter 1 ft deep (30 cms)

CROSS SECTION

20 ft (8 m)

Nest boxes (1 per 4 birds)

Tubular drinkers

20 ft (6 m)

Movable perch units

Tubular feeders

Divided sections 30 ft (9 m) x 20 ft (8 m) to take 200 birds

Access from front for cleaning

Fig. 14.3 Plans of covered straw yard

side facing in a southerly direction. The floor must be deeply strawed – about 0.3 m deep – and kept well topped-up throughout the laying period. The birds are given a generous space allowance of about 0.27 m² each. The equipment in the house consists of nest boxes for laying (one box to five birds), hanging feeders and drinkers and movable perch units for roosting. Artificial lighting is provided to help boost winter egg production.

Table 14.2 Performance data for poultry (adapted from Carnell 1983)

	Egg yield/ bird p.a. (hen housed average)	Birds/ person	Feed consumption/ per bird (kg p.a.)	Total costs/bird (£)
Battery cages	260	10 000	43	9.16
Deep-litter	250	8 000	42.5	9.36
Aviary	250	9 000	43	9.36
Straw yard	240	4 500	45.5	10.21
Free-range	220	1 800	46	11.75

The estimates given in this table by Carnell probably tend to underestimate both the egg production and the food consumption in the 'alternatives' to the cage systems, but are not in aggregate unreliable. It seems likely therefore that the 'alternative' systems increase the costs of production, as listed here, by a range of about 1% with good deep-litter housing to 20% with free-range.

Birds kept in this system are very active, spending a fair amount of time scratching in the straw, either searching for food or having dust-baths. Heavier types of bird producing brown eggs are ideal for straw yards since they settle much better and are less prone to vices such as feather-pecking. It is good practice to give a diet of meal, ad lib, and also scatter some grain on the floor each afternoon to give the birds variety and encourage their activity, as they scratch in the straw and keep it in good condition.

Table 14.3 shows the results of a recent trial completed in a covered straw yard, in which excellent productivity was achieved.

In a comparison by the author of results from covered straw yard birds with those kept in multi-bird cages in a fully

Table 14.3 Performance of birds in straw yard from 20–72 weeks at Gleadthorpe (1984–85) (from a personal communication by A. Hill, 1985)

Eggs/hen housed	282.8
Feed intake (g/bird/day)	138
Floor eggs (%)	1.00
Second quality eggs (%)	9.2
Mortality	3.1
Mean house temperature	11.2

Three types of pens were used and the building was a converted brick cattle shed. The results were extremely good in terms of production and health. Food consumption was (as anticipated) higher than in a controlled environment. The main problem found was in keeping the bedding in good 'shape' in the winter. Performance reflects great credit on the management and supervision of the birds – as a visitor I can testify to this.

controlled environment house, it was found that those in a straw yard performed as well with a slightly lower food consumption. The result, which was most surprising, was that the food conversion efficiency was marginally better in the straw yard than in the cage-house. As the straw yard has other advantages, it is worthy of more consideration. The advantages are that running costs are generally low, there are no fans and a minimum of artificial lighting, and there is nothing mechanical to go wrong. Straw is converted into a valuable manure, the quality of the eggs is good, being comparable to eggs from birds in a cage system, but the straw yard eggs being richer in colour and richer in B_{12}. There also appear to be no welfare problems.

It is interesting to speculate on the more efficient food conversion by chickens in the yard. It is noticeable that the birds are much better feathered in the yard, which probably improves their heat retention, and it is also found that they produce firmer droppings and spend less time in eating. It is possible that the caged bird eats and drinks more than it really requires because of the boredom of its existence, whilst straw yard birds spend time in activity on and in the litter and derive certain beneficial by-products from it. It should be noted, however, that the results for food consumption in straw yards found in my own studies have not been repeated by others, and further investigation is required on a wider scale to elucidate this finding.

The disadvantages of the straw yard system are that it requires more skill and care to operate than a cage arrangement, and cannot be very readily or cheaply automated. Some eggs may be unclean, depending on the state of the litter. It is a system unlikely to be favoured by the big operator but fits ideally into the mixed farms where the straw is produced locally and the litter can be returned to the land with great benefit. It is also certainly much easier to keep the environment calm and cosy in a small building such as a lean-to (monopitch) one than it is in a large and airy yard where cooler down-draughts are inevitable.

The aviary system

An aviary is essentially similar to a conventional deep-litter or slatted floor system but has the addition of extra floors of wire or slats (Fig. 14.4). The feeders, drinkers and nest boxes are provided on each of the floors and the various levels are interconnected by ladders which are able to take both the birds and their attendants.

The great advantage of this system is that it allows for the stocking density within the house to be much increased above that possible in an ordinary deep-litter house. This reduces the capital cost per bird, enables a warmer house temperature to be maintained more akin to that in a cage house, and thereby reduces food consumption. Also, because of the extra warmth,

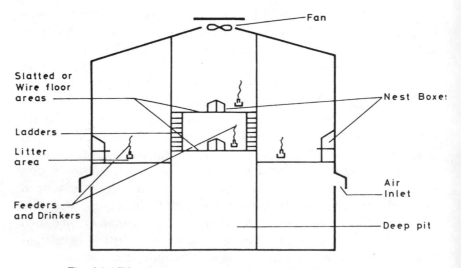

Fig. 14.4 Diagrammatic cross-section of Gleadthorpe Aviary

ventilation may be increased, thereby improving the litter conditions and generally eliminating condensation. Detailed studies on this system are currently being conducted at the Gleadthorpe Experimental Husbandry Farm of the Ministry of Agriculture, Fisheries and Food.

There is a widespread belief in both the research and commercial elements of the poultry industry that the aviary arrangement offers the best alternative for intensively housed birds which can be kept in controlled environment housing. Rather similar arrangements, known as 'percheries', are being developed which do not have the sophistication of the aviary but have the same aim of allowing birds access to various levels in the house, and also provide a littered area.

Modified free-range system

Traditional free-range systems allowed birds to roam freely over farm land at concentrations of up to 200 birds per acre. Birds roosted at night in simple sheds which also contained nest boxes. The problems of this system are very considerable, including excessive food usage, lost or dirty eggs, high labour costs, destruction of birds by predators, and often high mortality and disease incidence. However, a modified system is now practised (a plan of which is shown in Fig. 14.5), which overcomes some of these problems in the following way.

Fully insulated housing is provided which is capable of containing the birds entirely during poor weather, for example, deep snow, very hard frosts or in very wet conditions, all of which can be most harmful to the laying chicken. This housing may be permanent on a concrete base, or of a semi-permanent type, such as a semi-circular polythene 'poly-pen' which can be moved from time to time. Electricity must be provided to give lighting to keep up winter egg production. Thus this part of the house is essentially a deep-litter or covered straw yard.

An essential of free-range is that the birds must be able to go outside at all times during good weather and there should be palatable greenstuff for the birds to eat. Runs must be capable of being used in rotation and should be surrounded by fencing that is fox-proof. Birds must be shut up at night for safety, and also to keep them warm. It is highly dangerous to allow runs to become fowl-sick and therefore, once the pasture has been

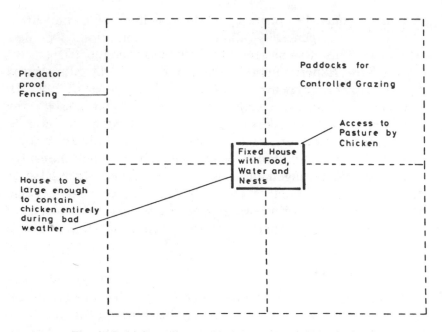

Fig. 14.5 A plan of a modified free-range chicken unit

denuded it should be vacated, ploughed up and reseeded. If pasture is used carefully for birds in a rotational programme there will be several benefits. The good health of the birds will be assisted, and the stocking density can be increased to well above 200 birds per acre in a particular run at any time; a factor of four times this will be acceptable and will also be of great benefit to the pasture before it is ploughed up.

It is probable that the use of modified free-range systems will have less application in temperate climates than in the warmer parts of the world, although in all areas there appears to be a definite place for them on well drained and dry land such as chalk downs, or sandy soil such as the Brecklands of Norfolk. Great credit is due to the pioneering farmers who are developing this arrangement by ingenious cost-saving methods. One farmer has recently built sheds with straw bales, using an internal aviary layout with multi-tiers of birds. With care, this sort of housing may last as long as ten years, with a very low capital input.

The welfare of birds in batteries

The question of the welfare of birds in battery cages still remains uncertain from the scientific angle. Dr. B.O. Hughes of the Poultry Research Centre at Edinburgh has carried out an extensive investigation for many years. He has asked the question, 'Can one make any quantitative recommendations as to the space requirement of a hen in a conventional battery cage?'. Statements have been made that hens should be given 450 cm^2 per bird, or 550 cm^2, or 600 cm^2, usually with little or no supporting evidence, and suggesting that it is an average value emerging from a committee whose members have offered a range of arbitrary figures. However, as we have seen, although it is impossible to offer a definitive value, there is now convincing evidence available from a number of different sources that the amount of space available in a typical battery cage is too small. There is a production response when hens are given more space; hens carrying out a limited range of basic activities cover an area greater than that which they are commonly offered. Some of the behaviour patterns which they perform in more spacious environments require much more space than the battery cage can provide, and they show a preference for spaces much larger than those they are generally offered. Thus the evidence, fragmentary though it is, all points in the same direction. Although one may safely conclude that more space is desirable, the evidence at present is such that no particular figure can be confidently recommended.

The second question is concerned with the strategy most likely to be effective in the future. It would seem to be inefficient to continue examining the space requirements for each of the multiplicity of behaviour patterns. The most economic approach would be to determine which behaviour pattern is most space-consuming, to establish the bird's needs to carry it out, and to delineate the spatial requirements for its performance. But this approach may be too simplistic. Of the main behaviour patterns let us look at three: wing-flapping, pre-laying behaviour, and avoidance of the 'personal space' of a dominant bird. Each of these may require the provision of a different sort of 'space'. Wing-flapping probably requires a firm-footing, a diameter at least equivalent to the bird's wing span, and an adequate (but unknown) ceiling height. Pre-laying behaviour may include elements of frustration unless the hen can find a suitable nest site, which may involve enclosure, separation from other birds, and an appropriate substrate. Avoidance of other birds' 'personal space' may require sufficient room to preserve adequate head-to-head distances and orientations. In certain circumstances this may be most readily achieved by the provision of multi-level environments.

A case could be made out for weighting the requirements in some fashion related to the frequency and duration of the behaviour pattern. Thus pre-laying behaviour, which occurs in most days, and may last up to 2 hours, might justify a higher priority than, say, wing-flapping, which only lasts a few seconds and occurs at a mean equivalent to about 10 times per day. The situation, therefore, is one in which value judgements must be made, the importance of each behaviour pattern being assessed and then a decision being arrived at as to how much space is necessary for its performance, sometimes in the face of inadequate or conflicting evidence.

Some kind of 'integrative' approach should perhaps be adopted, with each behaviour pattern making its own contribution to overall space requirements. There is no substitute for long-term, painstaking research describing the fowl's ethogram, establishing the need for each individual behaviour pattern, delineating its space requirements and designing a suitable environment to allow it to be carried out. Some of this work has been done, but much still remains to be tackled.

These are Dr. Hughes' conclusions in a recent paper, and they are written by a knowledgeable and compassionate veterinary investigator. There remains a need for this work to be vigorously pursued alongside the admirable endeavours of the commercial poultry industry, to find practical alternative systems to the battery cage.

References

Carnell, P. (1983) *Alternatives To Factory Farming*. London: Earth Resources Research Publication.

Hill, A. (1985) Personal communication. Ministry of Agriculture, Fisheries & Food, Gleadthorpe Experimental Husbandry Farm, Notts.

Hughes, B.O. (1983) 'Space requirements in poultry,' in *Farm Animal Housing and Welfare* pp. 121–127. The Hague: Martinus Nijhoff.

Further Reading

Aumaïtre, A. and Dantzer, R. (1984) 'Welfare of confined sows.' *Annals of Veterinary Research*, **15** (2) 149–309.

Baxter, S.H., Baxter, M.R. and MacCormack, J.A.D. (Eds.) (1983) *Farm Animal Housing and Welfare*. The Hague: Martinus Nijhoff.

Carnell, P. (1983) *Alternatives to Factory Farming*. London: Earth Resources Research Publications.

Dawkins, M. (1980) *Animal Suffering: The Science of Animal Welfare*. London: Chapman & Hall.

Duncan, I.J.H. (1981); 'Animal behaviour and welfare.' in J.A. Clark (Ed.) *Environmental Aspects of Housing for Animal Production*. pp. 455–470. London: Butterworths.

Farm Animal Welfare Programme (1984) Commission of the European Communities, Luxembourg.

Fraser, A.F. (1980) *Farm Animal Behaviour*. London: Baillière Tindall Ltd.

Houpt, K.A. and Wolski, T.R. (1982). *Domestic Animal Behaviour for Veterinarians and Animal Scientists*. Ames: Iowa State University Press.

Kilgour, R. and Dalton, C. (1984) *Livestock Behaviour. A Practical Guide*. London: Granada.

Signoret, J.P. (Ed.) (1982) *Welfare and Husbandry of Calves*. The Hague: Martinus Nijhoff.

Smith, D. (Ed.) (1983) *Indicators Relevant to Farm Animal Welfare*. The Hague: Martinus Nijhoff.

Sybesma, W. (Ed.) (1981) *The Welfare of Pigs*. The Hague: Martinus Nijhoff.

Webster, A.J.F. (1984) *Calf Husbandry, Health and Welfare*. London: Granada.

Wood-Gush, D.G.M. (1983) *Elements of Ethology*. London: Chapman & Hall.

Index